HMS
CAVALIER

HMS CAVALIER

DESTROYER 1944

Richard Johnstone-Bryden

Seaforth
PUBLISHING

First published in Great Britain in 2015 by
Seaforth Publishing,
Pen & Sword Books Ltd,
47 Church Street,
Barnsley S70 2AS

www.seaforthpublishing.com

British Library Cataloguing in Publication Data

A catalogue record for this book is available from the
British Library

ISBN 978 1 84832 226 4

Design by Stephen Dent
Deck layouts by Tony Garrett
Printed by Printworks Global Ltd, London & Hong Kong

CONTENTS

Half title: Looking aft from *Cavalier*'s stem.

Title pages: when *Cavalier* was brought to Chatham it was decided that she should be kept afloat to give the hull support even though she is permanently displayed within the Historic Dockyard's No 2 dry dock.

Above left: Bathed in the early morning sunlight *Cavalier* awaits the next influx of visitors.

FOREWORD

HMS CAVALIER IS PRESERVED AT THE HISTORIC
Dockyard Chatham in Kent as the National Destroyer
Memorial, commemorating the 142 Royal Navy
destroyers and over 11,000 men lost during the
Second World War.

Second World War destroyers were ubiquitous ships
that saw action across the world. *Cavalier* was one of
ninety-six war emergency destroyers built during the
Second World War. Based on the pre-war J class hull,
their high speed, armament and long range led them
to perform a wide range of duties, from working in
consort with the Navy's largest ships to escorting
convoys and supporting amphibious landings.

Modernised during the 1950s, *Cavalier* went on to
have a distinguished post-war career with the Royal
Navy – mostly in the Far East based at Singapore –
painted in the distinctive Light Admiralty Grey colour
she is depicted in today. She ended her service at
Chatham in 1972 with the title 'The Fastest Ship in the
Fleet', won the previous year in a race with HMS *Rapid*
in the North Sea – clearly demonstrating that she
retained her ability to make 32 knots, twenty-eight
years after her launch.

HMS *Cavalier* is now part of Chatham Historic
Dockyard Trust's collection of warships, berthed afloat
in No 2 Dry Dock, the Victory Dock on the site where

HMS *Victory* was built between 1759 and 1765. She is displayed alongside HMS *Gannet* (1878), a transitional period Victorian naval sloop, and HM Submarine *Ocelot* (1962), the last warship built for the Royal Navy at Chatham. Together with the archaeological remains of the *Namur*, a second rate ship of the line launched at Chatham in 1756, the three ships provide visitors with examples of ships built, maintained, repaired and refitted at Chatham Dockyard, and they demonstrate the transition from the timber-hulled sail-powered ships of the age of sail to the steam and steel of the nineteenth century, and on to the twentieth-century technology of submarines.

The Trust is particularly grateful to the National Heritage Memorial Fund and Heritage Lottery Fund whose support enabled HMS *Cavalier*'s future to be secured and brought to Chatham from Hebburn in 1999; to the first HMS *Cavalier* Trust and its volunteers who initially preserved her in Southampton and Tyneside, and to its present team, staff and volunteers who work tirelessly on her today to preserve her for the future.

Richard Holdsworth MBE
Director of Preservation and Education
Chatham Historic Dockyard Trust

THE **HISTORIC**
DOCKYARD
CHATHAM

1 | DESIGN AND CONSTRUCTION

SEVENTY-TWO YEARS AGO, WORK BEGAN ON A warship that was destined to become the nation's sole remaining wartime destroyer. The action-packed naval career of HMS *Cavalier* included the perilous Arctic Convoys of the Second World War, bombarding dissident Indonesian nationalists, quelling a mutiny in the Royal Indian Navy, supporting the hydrogen bomb tests on Christmas Island and becoming the fastest ship in the Fleet. Today, she is one of the principal attractions at The Historic Dockyard, Chatham and acts as a permanent memorial to more than 11,000 men who lost their lives in the 142 Royal Navy destroyers that were sunk during the Second World War.

The origins of the destroyer, as a type of warship, date back to the creation of the first vessels to carry Robert Whitehead's torpedo, which had been developed from a primitive, guided, self-propelled weapon devised by a retired Austrian naval officer, Captain Luppis, in 1866. Knowing that he did not have the technical capability to extract the full potential of his invention, Captain Luppis approached Robert Whitehead, who was running an engineering company in Fiume, to take on its development. Whitehead realised that the weapon would have to be capable of reaching its target underwater using a self-contained guidance system and propulsion for it to make a signif-

icant contribution to the future direction of naval warfare. Thus, within two years he had produced a weapon capable of carrying 18lb of dynamite at a depth of 15ft for a distance of 400 yards at 6 knots. This work attracted the support of the Austrian Government until a shortage of funds forced it to withdraw from the project, thereby creating an opportunity for the British Government to purchase the manufacturing rights for £15,000 in 1870. As part of the deal, Whitehead was given the use of a workshop at the Royal Laboratory, Woolwich Arsenal, to continue the weapon's development.

In 1873, work began on the Royal Navy's first torpedo-armed vessel HMS *Vesuvius* in Pembroke Dockyard. Capable of carrying up to ten Whitehead torpedoes, fired through a single submerged tube, she would have to rely on the element of surprise for her defence. To achieve this, near-silent engines were installed in the 260-ton vessel, while coke was burnt in the boilers, instead of coal, to significantly reduce the amount of smoke she produced. The fumes from the boilers were supposed to exit via side vents, as opposed to a conventional funnel. On completion, the 90ft twin screw *Vesuvius* could reach a speed of 9.7 knots and was used for experimental work.

As *Vesuvius* took shape, the Admiralty established a

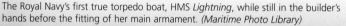

The Royal Navy's first true torpedo boat, HMS *Lightning*, while still in the builder's hands before the fitting of her main armament. *(Maritime Photo Library)*

The Royal Navy's first torpedo gunboat HMS *Rattlesnake*. *(Maritime Photo Library)*

torpedo committee. Its subsequent report recommended the construction of two main types of craft to carry the new weapon. Small, lightly built, high-speed torpedo-carrying craft for use in coastal and inshore waters were to be complemented by larger, seagoing torpedo vessels capable of operating with the Fleet.

Based on the design of a high-speed river launch, the 84ft HMS *Lightning* (TB No 1) was built by Thornycroft in 1877. She became the first of the Royal Navy's true torpedo boats when she was fitted with a pair of above-water tubes for Whitehead torpedoes in 1879. On the measured mile, *Lightning* reached a speed of 19 knots, which gave her the ability to launch an attack against an enemy warship at close range and swiftly escape. To counter this threat, torpedo gunboats were developed which combined a high speed and torpedo armament with light guns to destroy hostile torpedo boats. The first such craft to be built for the Royal Navy, HMS *Rattlesnake*, was completed by Laird's Birkenhead shipyard in 1887. Armed with a single 4in gun, six 3-pounder guns and four torpedo tubes, the 200ft *Rattlesnake* displaced 550 tons, yet could still reach a maximum speed of 19 knots.

The size of the torpedo boats and torpedo gunboats steadily increased in the coming years. However, the expanding gap in the speed of both types threatened the gunboat's future and led to the development of a new kind of vessel that could launch a torpedo attack against an enemy fleet at sea and eliminate hostile torpedo boats. To achieve this, the new ship would have to possess a combination of high speed and good seakeeping qualities, which led to the launching of the Royal Navy's first Torpedo Boat Destroyer (TBD), HMS *Havock*, by the Clydeside shipyard of Yarrow & Co in 1893. The initials TBD remained in use until the First World War to describe this type of warship, although it increasingly competed with the term destroyer which eventually became the accepted name for this kind of ship. With a top speed of 27 knots, *Havock*'s seaworthiness was evaluated during a 24-hour trial in the Bay of Biscay which proved to be a complete success. Armed with a 12-pounder, three 6-pounder guns, and three torpedoes, *Havock*'s design incorporated a turtleback fo'c'sle which became a distinctive feature of the early destroyers. The size and speed of her successors continued to rise, with 30 knots proving to be a difficult threshold to cross for those ships powered by reciprocating engines. Fortunately, an alternative form of propulsion had been pioneered by the British engineer Charles Parsons, who staged a dramatic demonstration of his steam turbine's potential during the Diamond Jubilee Naval Review at Spithead in 1897.

In a remarkable display of showmanship, the world's first steam turbine driven ship *Turbinia* suddenly appeared after HRH The Prince of Wales (later King Edward VII) had reviewed the fleet on behalf of Queen Victoria in HM Yacht *Victoria & Albert*. The 103ft experimental craft announced her arrival by weaving in between the anchored warships at speeds of up to 35 knots. With nothing to match *Turbinia*'s astonishing speed, the Navy were powerless to stop the antics of the uninvited guest. Not surprisingly, the embarrassment caused on this state occasion left quite an impression and prompted the Admiralty to act swiftly. Two years later, HMS *Viper* became the first steam turbine powered warship to be launched and was quickly followed by HMS *Cobra*. During her trials, *Viper* achieved a speed of 36.6 knots over a measured mile. Unfortunately, both ships suffered from a lack of longi-

The Royal Navy's first torpedo boat destroyer HMS *Havock*. *(Maritime Photo Library)*

The Royal Navy's first steam turbine powered warship HMS *Viper*. *(Maritime Photo Library)*

HMS *Arun* was a member of the River class, which were the first of the Royal Navy's destroyers to sport a raised fo'c'sle. This subsequently became a distinctive future of all its future destroyer designs until the early 1950s. *(Maritime Photo Library)*

tudinal strength, which caused their loss within two years and led to a temporary reversion to reciprocating engines for their immediate successors.

The 225ft River-class destroyers, completed between 1903 and 1905, were the first to incorporate a raised fo'c'sle which became a distinctive element of all future destroyer designs until the early 1950s. Their combination of improved strength of construction and the ability to operate in worse conditions compensated for a relatively modest top speed of 25 knots. The appointment of Admiral Sir John Fisher as First Sea Lord in October 1904 led to the development of three new types of destroyers and a swift reintroduction of steam turbines. Having set up a committee of designs, he informed them that the Board of Admiralty had decided to order ocean-going and coastal service destroyers. The ocean-going derivatives were to be armed with three 12-pounders, two torpedo tubes and capable of maintaining a speed of 33/34 knots at sea for 8 hours with a range of 1,500 miles at a speed of 16 knots, thereby enabling the 600-ton warships to be

deployed as part of the Fleet. The smaller coastal destroyers were to be armed with two 12-pounders and three torpedo tubes. With a maximum speed of 26 knots and a range of 1,000 miles at 15 knots, the coastal destroyers were envisaged as a cost-effective method of dealing with hostile torpedo boats in home waters. Thirdly, Fisher proposed the development of an experimental ship with a maximum ocean speed of at least 36 knots to be built to a moderate set of dimensions and cost. These latter requirements triggered the construction of the 2,170-ton HMS *Swift*. Armed with four 4in guns and two 18in torpedo tubes, her turbines boasted a combined output of 30,000 SHP which propelled her to a speed of 35 knots. Despite coming close to the operational aspect of her design brief, *Swift*'s £280,500 building costs considerably exceeded the financial objectives, thereby ruling out the ordering of any sister ships.

The Tribals were built in response to the criteria set out for the ocean-going destroyers, although they proved to be slightly larger than Fisher envisaged with a displacement of 875 – 1,000 tons. The first five ships were armed with five 12-pounder guns and two 18in torpedo tubes. The 12-pounder guns were replaced by two 4in guns on the final seven ships. In contrast, the coastal destroyers proved inadequate for their intended role and were reclassified as first-class torpedo boats.

The way in which destroyers were designed and operated changed during the First World War. Beforehand, the Admiralty allowed the individual specialist shipbuilders a degree of flexibility in how they met the design brief for each class of destroyer, to help foster new ideas that could improve their performance. This freedom was subsequently replaced by the

HMS *Tartar* was a member of the Tribal-class which was built to Admiral Fisher's requirements for an ocean-going destroyer. *(Maritime Photo Library)*

Admiralty's production of standard designs that had to be built to a rigid specification to create flotillas of destroyers with very similar performance and handling characteristics. On the outbreak of war, destroyers were used to attack the enemy's fleet with torpedoes and prevent similar attacks by their ships. Destroyers were subsequently used as a physical screen to deter submarine attacks and to escort convoys while some were converted for mine-laying and mine-sweeping.

The Royal Navy's V- and W-class destroyers of the First World War established the basic layout for the majority of destroyers that were launched by the world's navies during the 1920s and 1930s. Their key features included generous freeboard; two funnels; four guns, either 4in or 4.7in, dispersed in two single superimposed mountings fore and aft; two multiple torpedo-tube mountings and a displacement of approximately 1,250 tons.

As the First World War drew to a close, the German Navy pushed the boundaries of destroyer design by building a new class armed with 5.9in guns. Dubbed 'super destroyers,' the first two, *S113* and *V116,* were completed before the Armistice. With a displacement of 2,400 tons and the ability to reach a speed of 37 knots, they could successfully engage any existing destroyer and even act as a short range high-speed raider. The French, American, German and Japanese navies subsequently built their own 'super-destroyers' between the wars which prompted the development of the Royal Navy's Tribal-class destroyers in 1934. Armed with four twin 4.7in mountings, a four barrel pompom, two quadruple machine guns and one quadruple set of 21in torpedo tubes, the Tribals went on to perform with distinction in the Second World War. However, their size, cost and modest torpedo armament attracted criticism, leading to calls for a more economic derivative with a higher number of torpedo tubes and improved AA armament.

The Admiralty responded to these concerns in 1936 by developing the J or *Javelin* class. The adoption of longitudinal framing; the use of just two boilers, as

HMS *Mashona* was a member of the Royal Navy's interwar Tribal class. Built in response to the development of 'super-destroyers' by several navies, the Tribal class acquitted themselves with distinction in WWII. *(Maritime Photo Library)*

opposed to the trio fitted in the Tribals; the inclusion of six more 21in torpedo tubes and a reduction to six 4.7in guns dispersed in three twin mountings provided a surprisingly effective compromise which addressed the majority of the concerns that had been raised about the Tribals. With the prospect of a major conflict looking increasingly likely, the Admiralty chose the Javelin class in early 1939 as the basis for a standard hull design that would be used for war production. However, the long lead times for *Javelin's* twin 4.7in Mk XII guns on CP XIX mountings prompted a switch to four 4.7in Mk IX** guns on single CP XVIII mountings for the new standard destroyers. It was decided to capitalise on the inclusion of a lighter main armament by slightly reducing the length and beam of the hull, even though it limited the scope for future improvements once the ships entered service. Britain's declaration of war against Nazi Germany on 3 September 1939 triggered an order for the first batch of eight standard war-production destroyers. Each subsequent batch, known as an Emergency Flotilla, consisted of eight destroyers. The Admiralty continued to follow the pre-war alphabetical system for destroyer class-names with the 1st Emergency Flotilla being known as the O class. Once the first sixteen ships of the O and P classes had been ordered it was realised that the alterations to the hull design were, in fact, a false economy. Therefore, the hulls of the subsequent ninety-six ships were built to the same dimensions as *Javelin*. The revised hull also included a Tribal-style bow to reduce the amount of spray and a transom stern to improve their performance at higher speeds. These modifications had the added benefit of enabling an additional 125 tons of fuel to be carried thereby extending their range by 25 per cent.

The close-range armament fitted to individual ships varied according to the availability of specific weapon systems as each destroyer neared completion. Changes to the main armament were also introduced before the Admiralty ordered the Z class, otherwise known as the 10th Emergency Flotilla, on 12 February 1942. The four

One of the Royal Navy's V- and W-class destroyers, HMS *Wolvetine*. Developed during the First World War, they established the basic layout for the majority of destroyers that were launched by the world's navies during the 1920s and 1930s. *(Maritime Photo Library)*

HMS *Jackal*. The J-class destroyers were built as an economic alternative to the preceding Tribal class and went on to form the basis of the standard hull design that would be used for war-production (*Maritime Photo Library*)

4.7in guns of the earlier ships were replaced with a quartet of the recently developed 4.5in Quick Firing Mk IV gun, while two sets of quadruple 21in torpedo tubes superseded the pair of quintuple 21in torpedo tubes fitted to the earlier ships. Four days later, the Admiralty placed orders for the eight ships of the 11th Emergency Flotilla as repeats of the Z class. Having reached the end of the alphabetical system, the eight ships of the 11th Emergency Flotilla were initially allocated random traditional destroyer names. However, the Admiralty reviewed the situation before ordering the 12th Emergency Flotilla in July 1942 and decided that the 11th, 12th, 13th and 14th Emergency Flotillas would form part of a new C class. Each flotilla would be distinguished by the use of names starting with the letters CA, CH, CO and CR. Thus, the eight destroyers of the 11th Emergency Flotilla were allocated names beginning with the letters CA which led to *Pique* becoming the Royal Navy's first warship to be called *Cavalier*.

The contract for *Cavalier*'s construction, Admiralty Job Number J6099, was initially awarded to the Cammell Laird shipyard in Birkenhead. By November 1942, it became clear that Cammell Laird did not have the capacity to start work on the 363ft *Cavalier* and her sister ship *Carysfort* within the desired timescale. Therefore, both contracts were cancelled and reassigned to J Samuel White & Co on the Isle of Wight along with the allocated building materials. The move occurred at an interesting time in the yard's development as it prepared to make the transition from the building of riveted metal ships to welded metal ships. The change had been prompted by the extensive damage caused during the heaviest air raids carried out by the German Luftwaffe on Cowes in May 1942, in which 200 tons of high explosives and incendiaries were dropped. The valiant efforts of the gunnery crews on board the Polish destroyer ORP *Blyskawica* helped reduce the overall level of destruction inflicted on the town itself. By a fortuitous twist of fate, the warship still had her ammunition embarked while she underwent a refit in the yard where she had been built in the

mid-1930s. *Blyskawica* went on to serve in the Polish Navy until May 1976 and is now preserved in Gdynia.

Once the debris had been cleared away, J Samuel White & Co grasped the opportunity to rebuild its facilities so that they were ideally suited for the construction of large prefabricated welded sections that could be easily moved across to the appropriate slipway for final assembly. The new techniques were considered to be less physically demanding than riveting, which enabled women to be employed in the actual construction process, thereby increasing the pool of potential workers. The company decided to take a progressive approach to this transition by building *Cavalier* and *Carysfort* to a hybrid method of construction which incorporated the use of riveting and welding techniques. Based on the success of this work, the yard subsequently built the Royal Navy's first all-welded destroyer, HMS *Contest*.

The keel of the future HMS *Cavalier* was laid down without ceremony as shipyard number 1928 on 28 February 1943. Lady Glyn, whose husband was a director of J Samuel White, launched *Cavalier* on 7 April 1944. Afterwards, the lifeless hull was moved across to the western bank of the River Medina to be fitted out over the next eight months. By the time of her completion on 22 November 1944, *Cavalier*'s armament consisted of:

4 x 4.5in QF Mk IV guns
1 x twin Hazemeyer 40mm Bofors
2 x twin 20mm Oerlikons
3 x single 20mm Oerlikons
2 x quadruple 21in torpedo tubes
4 x depth charge throwers and 2 depth charge rails at the stern. A maximum of 108 depth charges were carried.

The contractor's sea trials, off the Isle of Wight, were interrupted on 28 December 1944 when the Free French frigate *L'Escarmouche* sent out a signal calling for help following the torpedoing of the troopship *Empire Javelin* off Cape Barfleur. Nearly 1,500 American soldiers, bound for mainland Europe, were embarked in the 11,650-ton Infantry Landing Ship as she started to sink by the stern. Fortunately, *Cavalier* had enough fuel to reach the stricken troopship and swiftly left the Solent at high speed, even though she still had several workers from J Samuel White & Co on board. In the meantime, *L'Escarmouche* went alongside to take on as many troops as possible before other ships, including *Cavalier*, arrived on the scene to provide further assistance. The subsequent search for the potential culprit proved inconclusive and *Cavalier* returned to the Solent the next day to continue with her trials.

2 | FIRST COMMISSION & MODERNISATION

ON COMMISSIONING, *CAVALIER* JOINED THE Home Fleet's 6th Destroyer Flotilla. In February 1945 she formed part of the screen for the escort carriers *Premier* and *Puncher* during three separate operations in Norwegian waters, Selenium, a strike on shipping; Shred, providing fighter cover for a mine-sweeping flotilla and Ground-sheet, an aircraft mine-laying strike. At the end of the month, *Cavalier* sailed from Scapa Flow together with the destroyers *Myngs* and *Scorpion* to reinforce the escort of the westbound Arctic Convoy RA64, which had been battered by hurricane force winds, torpedo bombers and U-boats. Against the odds, thirty-one of the convoy's thirty-four ships reached the safety of the Clyde on 1 March. However, the conditions endured by this particular convoy were so severe that all of the destroyers reported serious defects when they returned to Scapa Flow, with twelve requiring a refit or remedial work to be carried out in dry dock. *Cavalier*'s involvement was formally recorded by the award of her sole battle honour, 'Arctic 1945'. She spent the remaining months of the European war operating in the Western Approaches as an escort to several famous liners, including *Queen Mary*, *Queen Elizabeth* and *Aquitania* during the initial and final stages of their transatlantic trooping voyages.

After VE Day, *Cavalier* underwent a brief refit in Rosyth to prepare for service within the British Pacific Fleet. However, the dropping of the atomic bombs on Hiroshima and Nagasaki brought the conflict to a close before the destroyer left home waters and triggered her reassignment to the East Indies Station, where she arrived on 29 September 1945 to help re-establish order in the troubled region.

On 10 November, *Cavalier* participated in the occupation of Soerabaya, Java, by bombarding dissident Indonesian nationalists who had failed to respond to the Allied ultimatum to surrender. Three months later, she formed part of Force 64 to deal with unrest in the Royal Indian Navy by visiting Indian ports along the Indian West Coast between February and April, before heading back to the UK to pay off into the Reserve Fleet.

On 16 June 1946, *Cavalier* entered Portsmouth flying her paying-off pennant, to conclude her first commission. She subsequently sailed with a reduced ship's company to Gibraltar for a brief refit, before returning to Portsmouth where she joined the other destroyers and frigates awaiting their fate on the 'trot'

Cavalier returns to Portsmouth on 16 June 1946 to pay off into the Reserve Fleet. (*Wright & Logan / The National Museum of the Royal Navy*)

Cavalier while laid up on the 'trot' in Portchester Creek in the late 1940s. *(Conrad Waters' Collection)*

Cavalier alongside Thornycroft's Woolston shipyard during her 1955–57 modernisation. *(Maritime Photo Library)*

in Porchester Creek. To slow down the ship's deterioration while she was in reserve, *Cavalier* became one of the Navy's first warships to benefit from the new technique of encasing her weapons, radar aerials and other sensitive externally mounted equipment in PVC to create airtight 'cocoons.' For the majority of these ships, their stay in Porchester Creek would culminate in a one-way voyage to the breaker's yard. In contrast, *Cavalier* would sail again under her own power in 1957 after a refit in Portsmouth Dockyard, followed by an extensive two-year modernisation carried out in Thornycroft's Woolston shipyard.

The decision to install a Mark 6M Director Control Tower (DCT) and Remote Power Control (RPC) to the main armament, as well as two sets of triple-barrelled Squid anti-submarine mortars, triggered significant alterations to the ship's external profile. A new bridge, based on the design used for the *Daring* class, was installed complete with an enlarged operations room, ASDIC control room and a third wireless office. The removal of the X 4.5in mounting created enough space for two sets of triple-barrelled Squid ahead-throwing anti-submarine mortars, while the aft super-structure was extended forward and topped with a twin 40mm Bofors Mark V and a simple tachometric director Mk2 on a raised deckhouse. To compensate

for the additional weight incurred as a result of these changes, the depth charges, together with their associated rails and throwers, were removed along with the aft set of quadruple torpedo tubes. These changes led to *Cavalier*'s deep displacement rising from 2,510 tons to 2,675 tons, while her maximum speed dropped to 31 knots. The addition of 50 tons of permanent ballast underlined her limited scope for further improvements. In future, weight savings would have to be identified before any additional equipment could be fitted.

On completion of this modernisation, *Cavalier*'s armament consisted of:

3 x 4.5in QF Mk IV guns
1 x twin 40mm Bofors Mark V
2 x single 40mm Bofors 40/70
1 x quadruple set of 21in torpedo tubes
2 x 3 barrelled Squid anti-submarine mortars.

The rejuvenated destroyer's primary roles included screening heavy forces against attack by submarines, aircraft and light forces as well as attacking enemy light forces and trade. Her secondary roles consisted of attacking heavy ships with torpedoes and participating in combined operations.

Cavalier depicted in June 1958 following her modernisation. Note the lowered transducers for the Type 164 and Type 147 sonars. *(A D Baker III)*

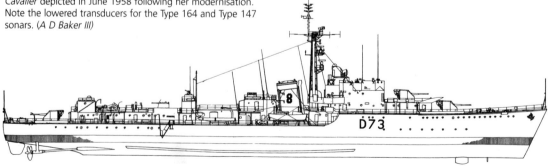

3 | THE FAR EAST FLEET

CAVALIER WAS RECOMMISSIONED ON 15 JULY 1957 as a replacement for *Comus* of the 8th Destroyer Squadron, Far East Fleet. During her outbound passage, she worked up off Portland and Malta before reaching Singapore on 31 October.

In April 1958 *Cavalier* was temporarily assigned to the Grapple Squadron stationed off Christmas Island in the South Pacific, to act as a weather- and guardship during the latest phase of the UK's hydrogen bomb trials codenamed Grapple Y. This series culminated in the dropping of a live weapon by Vickers Valiant B1 XD825 on 28 April off Christmas Island, which achieved an explosion of three megatons and proved to be the highest yield of all the British test devices used throughout the four separate sets of trials. On the day of the blast, *Cavalier* patrolled the exclusion zone, which had come into force forty-eight hours earlier, to prevent unauthorised shipping disrupting the trials or placing themselves in danger. As the countdown began, several members of the ship's company were on the upper deck, wearing anti-flash hoods, gloves, protective goggles and white overalls. They were told to sit down facing away from the blast with knees drawn up to their faces, which were to be covered by both hands. The men were instructed to keep their eyes firmly closed as the final seconds were counted down over the tannoy before the blinding flash of the

Cavalier's revised profile following her modernisation. (*Author's Collection*)

weapon's detonation, which occurred 53 seconds after its release by the Valiant flying at 46,000ft, at an altitude of 8,000ft. Afterwards, the ship's company were informed that they could open their eyes and turn to face the blast as the fireball generated an enormous mushroom cloud that extended to a height of approximately 50,000ft. Describing what they saw, an account in the ship's second commission book said, 'There was this great inferno in the sky, red and growing, evil and yet beautiful, bursting and growing white and huge – a monstrous white fungus.' The scientific results of this

Transferring stores between the Town class cruiser HMS *Newcastle* and HMS *Cavalier* in December 1957. (*Mike Fleet's Library*)

A close-up view of the changes that were carried out to *Cavalier*'s aft superstructure during her modernisation at Thornycroft's Woolston Shipyard. *(Mike Fleet's Library)*

test were so successful that plans for the dropping of a second live weapon were scrapped, thereby concluding the Grapple Y series of trials.

Following her release from the Grapple Squadron, *Cavalier*'s subsequent programme included participating in exercise Showboat, along with visits to Hong Kong and the Gulf, before returning to Singapore where her second commission concluded on 1 January 1959. By the late 1950s, the Far East Fleet's warships no longer had to return to the UK at the end of a commission to exchange their ship's company thanks to the increasing range and capacity of post-war passenger aircraft. Thus, the next ship's company of *Cavalier* flew out from the UK and recommissioned the destroyer on 9 January 1959, thereby saving the time and expense of the four-month round trip to conduct the change of personnel in a UK dockyard.

A rendezvous with HM Yacht *Britannia* on 21 February provided an interesting interlude between the usual programme of goodwill visits and exercises. *Cavalier* had been chosen to form part of the Far East Fleet's ocean escort for the yacht as she sailed towards Singapore with HRH The Duke of Edinburgh embarked during her second round-the-world tour. The rest of the group consisted of the cruiser *Ceylon*, the destroyer *Cheviot*, along with the frigates *Chichester*, HMAS *Queenborough* and HMAS *Quiberon*. Under the tactical command of Captain F R Twiss in *Ceylon*, the ships fired a 21-gun salute as they approached the yacht in the Malacca Strait before steaming past *Britannia* at 22 knots while manning the rail and

cheering His Royal Highness. On completion of these exciting manoeuvres, the escort took up station in formation astern of the yacht for the remainder of the passage to Singapore. At the end of the Duke of Edinburgh's visit to Singapore, the same group of warships escorted the yacht as she set sail for Borneo on 25 February. They subsequently parted company with *Britannia* during the night and resumed their normal duties.

A four-month refit in Singapore, followed by exercise Jet, preceded *Cavalier*'s diversion to Addu Atoll at the beginning of August in response to unrest on the island of Gan in the Maldives. She spent the rest of the month acting as guardship for the RAF's facilities until *Caprice* relieved her on 29 August.

Within a few hours of arriving in Hong Kong on 22 September, *Cavalier* received orders to sail at once to the assistance of the merchant ship *Taichungshan* which had been shelled by Chinese Nationalists off Amoy. Fortunately, there were no casualties and the damaged merchant ship managed to reach Hong Kong without assistance under the watchful eye of *Cavalier*. The destroyer's participation in the next month's exercise with the US 7th Fleet off the west coast of the Philippines, as *Centaur*'s plane guard, was cut short by the unwelcome discovery of oil pouring out of a split in the warship's side. Following repairs in the Whampoa commercial dry dock in Kowloon, the final six months of the commission included visits to Japan, Gan, Australia, the Philippines and Singapore. As the commission drew to a close, *Cavalier* took part in an exercise organised by the South East Asia Treaty Organisation (SEATO), Sea Lion, in April 1960. *Cavalier*'s performance caught the attention of the American commander who sent the following message to the ship at the end of the exercise: 'Upon termination as a task unit commander of which *Cavalier* was part, may I express my pleasure at having so smart a ship to work with. Excellence in gunnery envoked the admiration of all.' The words provided a fitting finale to the third commission, which concluded following *Cavalier*'s return to Singapore on 13 May.

The next ship's company were flown out in time for a brief handover period with their predecessors prior to recommissioning *Cavalier* on 24 June 1960. Afterwards, *Cavalier* pursued her familiar routine of goodwill visits and participating in exercises. While en route to Australia for a series of goodwill visits in September 1960, the ship's company enjoyed a brief respite from their normal duties when they received a visit from King Neptune for a customary crossing-the-line ceremony. During the course of the festivities, those visiting His Oceanic Majesty's realm for the first time, along with a select band of individuals who had been summoned to appear before the court, were shaved by the barber and ducked by the bears in the temporary canvas pool which had been rigged amidships.

The goodwill visits continued after Australia with stops in Guam and Japan before *Cavalier* underwent a short refit in Singapore from December 1960 to February 1961. Afterwards, *Cavalier* sailed for one of SEATO's largest exercises, Pony Express, which took place in April 1961 off North Borneo in the South China Sea. A fleet of sixty warships, including *Cavalier*, gathered for the exercise which involved 20,000 naval personnel and 6,000 troops from six nations. The fourth commission concluded with a full speed trial on the way back to Singapore in November 1961 where *Cavalier* paid off and her ship's company flew back home in two batches just in time for Christmas.

Sadly, their successors had to leave their families at the worst time of year as they flew out to Singapore to join *Cavalier* ahead of the commissioning ceremony on 11 December. The destroyer sailed the next day to begin her work-up and spent Christmas in Hong Kong. The New Year's programme included the SEATO exercise Jet 62 and a visit in company with *Centaur* to Aden in March for ten days of promotional work in support of the UK's defence industry during Aden armed forces week, which concluded the carrier's latest deployment east of Suez. However, before *Centaur* could head north, she had to wait for *Ark Royal* to complete her southbound transit of the canal. This simple precaution ensured that the Royal Navy would always have at least one carrier available to deal with

any emergencies east of Suez, even in the event of the canal's sudden closure. *Cavalier* also waited for *Ark Royal*'s arrival and escorted her to Singapore. Afterwards, *Cavalier* visited Korea and Japan in company with HMS *Carysfort* before undergoing a short refit in Singapore from July to September.

While on passage to Fremantle for the Empire Games in November, *Cavalier* was alerted to an unfolding emergency on board the American research vessel *Horizon,* located some 1,200 miles away in the Pacific. One of her sailors was suffering from internal bleeding and pneumonia. In a fortuitous twist of fate, the Squadron's surgeon was embarked in *Cavalier* at the time, so the destroyer set off at high speed to rendezvous with *Horizon*. On the way, Surgeon Lieutenant Alistair Scott-Brown liaised with the American ship over the radio about the patient's condition. When the two ships met, the rough conditions ruled out a jackstay transfer, thereby forcing the patient to be brought across to *Cavalier* in the sea boat – a hazardous operation that took one and a half hours to complete. Once the sailor was on board, *Cavalier* embarked on the 1,600 mile passage to Fremantle, taking on fuel from RFA *Wave Ruler* on the way. On arrival, the waiting ambulance took the American sailor to the nearby hospital for further treatment.

The pace quickened again after the Australian visit, owing to an armed rebellion in Brunei, Sarawak and North Borneo on 8 December 1962 against the formation of Malaysia. *Cavalier* received orders to proceed to Singapore at high speed and embark a detachment of troops drawn from a combination of the Royal Marines, the Ghurkhas and the Queen's Own Highlanders complete with their vehicles and stores. To increase the amount of available deck space, the sole remaining set of quadruple torpedo tubes was temporarily landed in Singapore. On reaching Brunei, *Cavalier* disembarked the troops and acted as a communications HQ ship while members of ship's company guarded 400 captured rebels ashore until the destroyer was relieved by the cruiser HMS *Tiger*.

Having spent Christmas and the New Year in Singapore, *Cavalier* began her long voyage home by sailing to Hong Kong for a five-day visit, before heading to the South Pacific to take on the role of royal search and rescue ship while the Queen and the Duke of Edinburgh flew across the Pacific in a Boeing 707 to Fiji, where they were due to join HM Yacht *Britannia* for their tour of Australia and New Zealand. Afterwards, *Cavalier* underwent a brief self-maintenance period within New Zealand's Devonport Dockyard before resuming her homeward passage via Tahiti, Christmas Island, Pearl Harbor, San Diego,

The difference between the original riveted construction of the hull and the new welded bow that was fitted following *Cavalier*'s collision with the tanker *Burgan* on 21 May 1964 can clearly be seen.

Mexico, and El Salvador. Following her transit of the Panama Canal, *Cavalier* spent over a week on patrol off Haiti during the island's revolution. *Cavalier*'s relief by HMS *Caprice* enabled her to take on fuel in Bermuda, before heading across the Atlantic via Ponta Delgada in the Azores to Portsmouth, where she arrived on 26 May 1963 to conclude her six-year tour of duty in the Far East. Two days later, *Cavalier* steamed round to Chatham Dockyard to pay off into reserve and await a decision on her future.

On 21 May 1964, *Cavalier* lost the first 30ft of her bows in a collision with the 17,905-ton Liberian-registered tanker *Burgan* in the English Channel, while under tow from Chatham to Gibraltar for her next refit. Fortunately, there were no casualties among the destroyer's skeleton crew and the virtually unscathed *Burgan* continued with her voyage to Rotterdam.

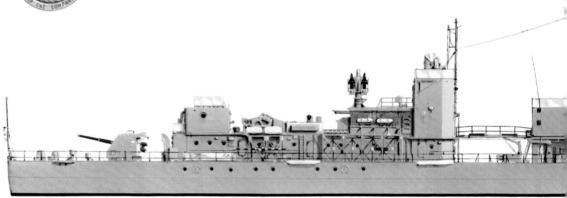

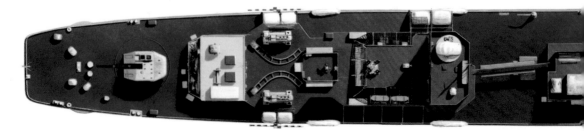

However, *Cavalier* had to be towed stern first to Portsmouth Dockyard for a new bow to be fitted.

On reaching Gibraltar, work began on the replacement of the twin 40mm Bofors Mark V mounting with the close range surface-to-air Guided Weapons System Mk20 (GWS20) Seacat missile system. The four-round launcher was fitted in the position previously occupied by the 40mm Bofors. The forward end of the aft superstructure was built up in the form of a 'tower' to accommodate the magazine for the missiles, while its upper deck provided a suitable location for the Seacat's director. The remaining set of 21in quadruple torpedo tubes was permanently landed to compensate for the weight of the new magazine.

Cavalier recommissioned in 1966 for a brief spell with the Home Fleet before sailing for the Far East in May 1967, via the Cape of Good Hope, owing to the closure of the Suez Canal by the Six Day War between Israel and Egypt. Her last deployment east of Suez included two Beira patrols. This long running commitment was instigated by the British Government in 1966 to enforce the United Nations oil embargo against Rhodesia, now known as Zimbabwe, following the declaration of independence from the UK by its Prime Minister, Ian Smith, on 11 November 1965. The first patrols were carried out by the Royal Navy's fleet carriers *Ark Royal* and *Eagle,* which used their air groups to detect tankers that might be heading to the Portuguese port of Beira to supply oil via its pipeline to the landlocked Rhodesia, thereby breaking the United Nations embargo. The Royal Navy maintained the patrol until 25 June 1975, when Mozambique gained its independence and agreed not to supply oil to Rhodesia.

Cavalier's final configuration following the fitting of the GWS20 Seacat missile system. (*Tom Brittain / Profile Publications Ltd*)

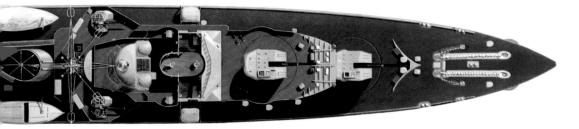

4 | HOME WATERS & THE MEDITERRANEAN

CAVALIER SHOULD HAVE PAID OFF FOR DISPOSAL following her return to the UK on 30 May 1968. However, the Royal Navy was suffering from a shortage of available escorts, which led to a further reprieve. Thus she spent the remainder of her active service operating in home waters and the Mediterranean. *Cavalier* recommissioned for the last time in Portsmouth on 6 March 1970 with a ship's company consisting of twelve officers and 180 men. Although her long career was finally drawing to a close, the veteran destroyer continued to fulfil a varied programme of commitments, which included participating in 'meet the Navy', Navy Days, NATO exercises, fishery protection patrols, conducting surveillance of the Soviet Fleet, transporting ex-concentration camp victims to a reunion in Alderney, as well as acting as plane guard for HMS *Ark Royal* and guardship for Gibraltar. Along the way she visited thirty-two ports in nine countries and clocked up another 169,242 miles.

Her second spell of plane guard duties in support of HMS *Ark Royal* took an unexpected twist on the night of 8 September 1970 owing to the outbreak of a fire onboard the coaster *St Brandon* in the Bristol Channel. Flag Officer Plymouth instructed the carrier to co-ordinate the naval involvement in the rescue operation. Shortly afterwards, *Cavalier* received orders to proceed at best speed towards the stricken vessel's position. While on her way, news came through that the French trawler *Henri Callogh* had rescued *St Brandon*'s crew. Despite this development, *Cavalier* pressed on through the deteriorating conditions and located the blazing coaster early the next morning, about 40 miles west of Lundy Island. *St Brandon* still posed a risk to nearby shipping, so *Cavalier* remained on station to warn approaching vessels and provide the Coastguard with occasional updates about her status. By daybreak, the fires were dying down and the hull still appeared to be remarkably sound, thereby raising the possibility of towing *St Brandon* to a safe haven. However, *Cavalier* would have to wait for an improvement in the weather before a boarding party could attempt to secure a tow line between the two ships. In the meantime, the

Cavalier approaches the Forth Railway Bridge. Having spent the majority of her service in the Far East, *Cavalier* spent her final four years in commission in home waters and the Mediterranean. *(Ambrose Greenway)*

winds strengthened to Force 11, which forced the destroyer to seek shelter in the lee of Lundy Island and track *St Brandon* by radar overnight as she drifted eastwards up the Bristol Channel.

When the winds eased slightly to Force 10 on the morning of 10 September, *Cavalier* caught up with the coaster again and a boarding party overcame the hazardous conditions to secure a tow line. By mid-morning the two ships were heading towards Milford Haven at three knots. They were briefly parted in the afternoon, by which time the wind had moderated to Force 8. Within an hour, the tow had been re-established, which enabled the ships to resume their sedate passage to Milford Haven, where they arrived at 0400 on 11 September. Once alongside, *Cavalier* turned over *St Brandon* to the custody of the Resident Naval Officer Pembroke Dock, thereby initiating the process to claim a salvage award to be distributed among everyone serving in the ship during the recovery operation. With a combined value of £167,000 for the coaster and her cargo, it proved to be one of the largest salvage claims to have been lodged on behalf of a Royal Navy warship. The amount paid to each individual was determined by the number of shares they were entitled to as a result of their seniority on board, as follows: sixty shares for the commanding officer, ten for a chief petty officer, eight for a petty officer, six for a leading seaman, five for an able seaman and three for an ordinary seaman.

Afterwards, the destroyer resumed her plane guard duties for the rest of *Ark Royal*'s work-up before accompanying the carrier during exercise Northern Wedding. An unexpected encounter with the frigate HMS *Rapid* resulted in an exchange of cheeky signals that triggered a race to settle which one could claim to be the fastest in the Fleet. Contrary to initial impressions, the contest was to be evenly matched owing to *Rapid*'s origins as a wartime R-class destroyer. Even

Cavalier could still achieve an impressive 31.8 knots until she paid off for the last time in 1972. *(Ambrose Greenway)*

though she had been converted into a Type 15 anti-submarine frigate in the early 1950s, *Rapid* still retained her original underwater profile and machinery. Neither ship could be spared from their immediate duties, so the competition had to be delayed until a suitable date could be found on which they could conduct their annual full power trial in company. A close inspection of their respective programmes revealed an opportunity for this to take place in the North Sea on 6 July 1971. Having spent the previous three weeks on fishery protection duties off Iceland and the North Cape, *Cavalier*'s marine engineers were confident about their chances against a 'mere frigate'.

The media turned out in force to cover 'the great race' on a perfect summer's day. As the final countdown commenced, both ships weighed anchor and carried out a series of high speed manoeuvres that culminated in their crossing the starting line abeam at 30 knots. As soon as the gun had been fired, the chief of the watch in *Cavalier*'s engine room wound open the mighty throttle wheels to extract every last ounce of power. *Rapid* drew ahead by two cables in the first half-hour, which sparked a frantic round of fine adjustments by *Cavalier*'s marine engineers to help tip the balance in the destroyer's favour. As the gap closed,

A fine view of *Cavalier* as her active service draws to a close. *(Ambrose Greenway)*

On 6 July 1971 *Cavalier* and the former wartime destroyer HMS *Rapid* held their annual full power trial in company to see which one could claim to be the fastest in the fleet. Billed as 'the great race', it attracted the attention of the media, who turned out in force to cover the event. In this view *Cavalier* is seen from the deck of her competitor. *(Ambrose Greenway)*

Rapid lifted a safety valve towards the end of the two-hour trial and appeared to signal the end of the race. However, both ships pressed on until the firing of the green Very light, by which time *Cavalier* had reached a maximum speed of 31.8 knots to narrowly win the 64 mile race by just 30 yards. The tight margin was a tremendous testament to the dedication of the marine engineering departments in both ships, who managed to achieve such a high performance from the elderly warships. However, time was finally running out for *Cavalier* as a shortage of spares for her ageing equipment forced the Navy to withdraw her from service. By

the time *Cavalier* returned to Chatham to pay off for the last time on 6 July 1972 she had steamed 564,140 miles. Although *Cavalier* was the last of the Royal Navy's wartime destroyers to remain in front line service, her sister ship, HMS *Caprice*, became the last of their type to remain in commission and finally paid off on 2 April 1973. Capable of returning to front line service at short notice, HMS *Caprice* spent her final two years in commission attached to the Royal Naval Engineering College Manadon, Plymouth, as a sea-going training ship for engineer officers. She was subsequently sold for scrap in 1979.

5 | INITIAL PRESERVATION

THE TWILIGHT OF *CAVALIER*'S NAVAL CAREER coincided with the successful preservation of the light cruiser HMS *Belfast* in the Pool of London. On 21 October 1971, *Belfast* was officially opened to the public and became the first warship to be saved for the nation since Lord Nelson's flagship HMS *Victory* was preserved in 1922. This ambitious scheme proved that warships can be successfully turned into heritage attractions, providing that enough funding has been secured, along with a prominent berth, a long-term maintenance plan and a project team that has the ability to exploit any commercial opportunity. Such schemes cannot be conjured up on the spur of the moment and require a reasonable period of time to gain the necessary momentum. Having appreciated this latter factor, some of the ship's officers set about trying to highlight *Cavalier*'s rich heritage as her naval career drew to a close, in the hope of attracting enough influential backers who could ensure the veteran destroyer's long term preservation. Their efforts soon caught the attention of Admiral of the Fleet Earl Mountbatten, who had commanded the ill-fated destroyer HMS *Kelly* which inspired the film *In Which we Serve*, the chairman of the HMS *Belfast* Trust, Rear Admiral Morgan Morgan-Giles, and *The Daily Telegraph*'s naval correspondent Desmond Wettern. In December 1971, *Cavalier* was officially approved for disposal thereby formally triggering the battle for her future. The Navy agreed to restrict its de-storing process to the removal of the most sensitive items of equipment until her ultimate fate had been determined. This commitment significantly increased her chances of survival for two reasons. First, it created the opportunity for a heritage organisation to achieve the highest levels of authenticity in the way that it presented *Cavalier* to the public. Secondly, it reduced the cost, along with the physical challenge, of opening *Cavalier* to the public by ensuring vital systems such as the fire main remained intact.

The HMS *Cavalier* Trust was subsequently set up under the chairmanship of Rear Admiral Douglas Parker, who had commanded *Cavalier*'s sister ship HMS *Cavendish*, to preserve *Cavalier* as a memorial to those who had served in the Royal Navy's destroyers during the Second World War. With the enthusiastic support of Lord Mountbatten, it took the trust five years to raise £215,000 to purchase the ship and convert her into a floating museum. As the money started to come in, the trust searched for a suitable mooring. The Government refused to offer a berth within one of the dockyards, while the only options offered by the Port of London were too far from the main tourist routes. Sadly, the timescales associated with Greenwich Borough Council's potentially promising invitation did not tie in with the deadlines that were being set by the Ministry of Defence for *Cavalier*'s removal from Chatham. Eventually, Southampton City Corporation offered the trust the use of a berth at Southampton's Mayflower Park. This news, coupled with the raising of £65,000, enabled the trust to purchase *Cavalier* on 4 October 1977. A week later, naval tugs towed her round from Chatham to Portsmouth to be inspected in dry dock before the Government officially handed her over to the HMS *Cavalier* Trust on 21 October 1977. On completion of the formalities, Lord Mountbatten joined *Cavalier* as she was towed the short distance from Portsmouth to Southampton amid a blaze of publicity. Even though her arrival represented a significant milestone, the trust still had to raise a further £150,000 to pay for her conversion into a floating museum. Five years later, the trust achieved its objectives and officially opened *Cavalier* to the public in August 1982. With hopes of attracting 200,000 visitors per year, the veteran's future seemed assured. However, trouble lay ahead, as the scrapman's blow torch appeared to be waiting in the wings on more than one occasion. Within a year of opening to the public, the trust was facing financial difficulties. *Cavalier*'s location proved to be too far away from the city centre, with the ship failing to attract enough visitors to cover her operating costs.

In a bid to revive its flagging fortunes, the trust accepted an offer from the owners of the recently completed Brighton Marina for *Cavalier* to form its centrepiece. Thus the final visitors were admitted onboard the veteran destroyer in Southampton towards the end of October 1983. Within a month she had been moved along the south coast to her new home, where work began to strip down the aft messes on 3 deck. Although the purpose of this work has been lost to the mists of time, it is assumed that the trust hoped either to convert them back to their original configuration as a contrast to the modernised mess decks up forward, or transform the space into a museum gallery dedicated to the ship's history. Sadly, the destroyer did not fare any better in her new home.

Once again, she was too far away from the main tourist routes and only attracted an average of 1,000 visitors per week, which failed to cover her long term costs. This downward spiral triggered the trust's collapse in 1987 and left its bankers, Messrs Coutts & Co, with the liability of *Cavalier*'s disposal.

Fortunately, these difficulties coincided with the development of ambitious plans by South Tyneside Metropolitan Borough Council to create a National Shipbuilding Exhibition Centre on the site of the former Hawthorn Leslie shipyard in Hebburn on South Tyneside. The council had already bought the shipyard and decided to purchase *Cavalier* for £70,000 as the centrepiece for its proposed attraction. Following her arrival on the Tyne, *Cavalier* was berthed on Hawthorn Leslie's outfitting quay while the council refined its plans and applied for grants to implement the scheme. A steady trickle of visitors made their way to Hebburn to explore the destroyer until she had to be closed owing to the development of a list which forced her to be swiftly moved into the adjacent disused dry dock in 1994. Even though she subsequently reopened to the public on an occasional basis, the number of visitors fell into terminal decline. Before long, access was restricted to pre-booked organised groups as *Cavalier* was left to languish in the derelict dry dock. Meanwhile, the council's hunt for funding proved

equally fruitless. As a last resort, having secured 40 per cent of the required funding for the scheme from other sources, the council submitted an application to the Heritage Lottery Fund (HLF) for a grant of £4.2million in September 1995. HLF's rejection of this bid in April 1996 effectively torpedoed the council's plans for the National Shipbuilding Exhibition Centre and threw *Cavalier*'s future in doubt once more. After discounting the possibility of operating the destroyer as a stand-alone tourist attraction, the council decided to dispose of *Cavalier* in December 1996.

A proposal by Star Cruises Properties emerged as the only serious contender. Controversially, it wanted to move *Cavalier* to Malaysia's Port Kelang to become part of a museum of shipping. However, the HMS *Cavalier* Association, whose membership consists of those who had served in the ship, strongly objected to the proposal, stating that Malaysia was an inappropriate final destination for the veteran destroyer. Although the company managed easily to secure an export licence for *Cavalier* from the Department of Trade and Industry (DTI) on 31 July 1997, it had not anticipated the potential problems of securing an additional export licence from the Department for Culture, Media and Sport. The requirement for this second licence had been prompted by *Cavalier*'s status as a means of transport that was over fifty years old and worth in

Cavalier alongside the former Hawthorn Leslie shipyard on the Tyne. Although South Tyneside Metropolitan Borough Council's ambitious plans for the veteran destroyer were ultimately unsuccessful, it did provide her with a safe haven at a time when she would otherwise have been scrapped. This in itself was a significant contribution to the ship's long-term preservation, ensuring she survived before finding a permanent home in the heart of The Historic Dockyard Chatham. (*Ambrose Greenway*)

excess of £39,000. In a bid to avoid a further round of scrutiny, the Malaysian company changed the £750,000 value it declared for *Cavalier* to the DTI to a nominal £1. Not surprisingly, such a dramatic change in valuation raised further questions. These difficulties, coupled with vocal opposition from the veterans, persuaded Star Cruises Properties to withdraw its offer in January 1998. The council was left in an impossible situation. On the one hand, it did not want to be responsible for the destruction of an important element of the nation's maritime heritage, yet it could not continue to justify spending at least £30,000 per year on her basic maintenance at the expense of other services for its residents. In attempt to force the issue, the council declared that it would consider selling *Cavalier* for scrap within three months unless an alternative serious bidder came forward. The race was on to find a new home before the destroyer's luck finally ran out.

Cavalier's fate was finally resolved during her time in this dry dock in the former Hawthorn Leslie shipyard in Hebburn. *(Chatham Historic Dockyard Trust: Photographic Collection PHA.16714)*

6 | RETURN TO CHATHAM

IT IS EASY TO CRITICISE THE WAY IN WHICH South Tyneside Metropolitan Borough Council handled *Cavalier*'s preservation. In reality, it deserves enormous credit for having the courage to accept the challenge of trying to develop a viable long-term solution for the ship at a time when she would have otherwise been broken up for scrap. While there is no denying that *Cavalier*'s overall condition seriously deteriorated during her time on the Tyne, including the theft of several fixtures and fittings, the council played a significant role in her long-term survival by safeguarding the ship until she could be preserved elsewhere.

The timing of *Cavalier*'s latest difficulties coincided with a fortuitous turns of events in Chatham. When the Government closed the Dockyard and Naval Base at Chatham in 1984 it split the site into three sections. One section was turned into a commercial port that is now run by Medway Ports, another became a mix of commercial, leisure and residential sites, while the third was transferred to the Chatham Historic Dockyard Trust to secure its long term preservation for the benefit of the public. The trust's eighty-acre site includes approximately one hundred buildings and structures, of which forty-seven are scheduled as Ancient Monuments. It is considered to be the world's best preserved dockyard from the age of sail and attracts approximately 160,000 visitors every year. At the time of its founding by the Government, the majority of the trust's historic buildings were in a poor state of repair. The cost of making all of them wind- and weathertight was estimated to be in the region of £20 million, to which the Government contributed £11 million when it transferred the site to the trust. The scale of these buildings together with their poor condition, historical signifi-

cance and location in the post-industrial Medway towns, where unemployment was running at 27 per cent following the Navy's withdrawal, made the challenge of creating a sustainable future for the site via the achievement of the twin charitable goals of preservation and education a daunting one by any standards.

In addition to opening the Historic Dockyard to the public, the trust started attracting commercial tenants for several of its historic buildings and offering long-term leaseholds for the houses located within its site. The commercial tenants included a ship repair company which took over two of the Historic Dockyard's trio of dry docks. The company's demise in 1997 created an opportunity for the Trust to move HM Submarine *Ocelot*, the last warship to be built by the Dockyard for the Royal Navy, from a nearby basin for display alongside the Victorian sloop HMS *Gannet* and acquire a third historic ship. Representatives of the HMS *Cavalier* Association and the Friends of HMS *Cavalier* approached the trust to ask if they would provide a berth to secure *Cavalier*'s future and enhance the Historic Dockyard. The chairman, Admiral Sir Nicholas Hunt, responded by offering the use of the recently 'liberated' No 2 dock, providing that the funding for her acquisition and restoration could be secured.

As *Cavalier*'s future hung by a thread, her plight was brought to the attention of the House of Commons Culture, Media and Sport Select Committee. Its chairman, The Rt Hon Gerald Kaufman, arranged for the issue to be brought before the committee during a special one-day hearing in the House of Commons on 17 February 1998. Despite sceptical comments about the case for *Cavalier*'s preservation, as well as its viability, by the Department for Culture, Media and Sport, the Heritage Lottery Fund (HLF), the National Historic Ships Committee and the Imperial War Museum, the committee's subsequent report concluded that *Cavalier* 'should and can be saved'. The committee was particularly impressed by the argument put forward by the HMS *Cavalier* Association and the Friends of HMS *Cavalier* Trust that as the last surviving example of the Royal Navy's wartime destroyers she should become a memorial to those who lost their lives at sea in the Second World War. It went on to make a series of recommendations to increase the chances of her salvation.

Within weeks, a consortium had been formed by the HMS *Cavalier* Association, the Friends of HMS *Cavalier*

Cavalier is brought home to the Medway on 16 May 1999. (*Chatham Historic Dockyard Trust: Photographic Collection PHA.16725*)

Cavalier is eased into her final resting place in the heart of the Historic Dockyard, Chatham. Before leaving the Tyne, the destroyer was repainted in a dark shade of grey which provided a sharp contrast to how she appeared during her final years in commission. Thus, in keeping with the Historic Dockyard's policy of presenting *Cavalier* in her final operational guise, she was subsequently repainted to match the colours that were used before she paid off in 1972. *(Chatham Historic Dockyard Trust: Photographic Collection PHA.23050)*

Trust, the Chatham Historic Dockyard Trust and Medway Council to establish the feasibility of bringing the ship back to her former home port. The HLF approved a grant to pay for this work, which confirmed the viability of preserving *Cavalier* as part of a three-ship attraction at Chatham alongside HM Submarine *Ocelot* and HMS *Gannet*. However, before the plans could proceed any further, the consortium set up a new body, HMS *Cavalier* (Chatham) Trust Ltd, to act as the applicant for potential sources of funding and become the destroyer's owner if these initiatives proved successful. Chaired by a former chief executive of English Heritage, Mrs Jane Sharman, the HMS *Cavalier* (Chatham) Trust Ltd applied for charitable status and was subsequently registered with the central Charities Commission as Charity No 1074598.

In the meantime, events continued to move swiftly with the National Heritage Memorial Fund (NHMF) awarding a grant of £830,000 towards *Cavalier*'s preservation on 26 June 1998. Three months later, this amount was increased to £961,000 and supplemented by the HLF's agreement in principle to grant a further £600,000 towards the shoreside interpretation of *Cavalier, Ocelot* and *Gannet*.

In view of these encouraging developments, South Tyneside Metropolitan Borough Council continued to cover *Cavalier*'s expenses, despite the rejection of an application for HLF funding to pay for emergency repairs to the gate of the dry dock in which the destroyer was located. The council was concerned that the leaking gate was in danger of imminent failure, which could cause further damage to *Cavalier*. Fortunately, the gate remained in place until the time came to ease her out of the dry dock. On receiving confirmation of the second tranche of funding from the HLF and NHMF, the HMS *Cavalier* (Chatham) Trust Ltd proceeded with the acquisition of *Cavalier* from South Tyneside Metropolitan Borough Council for £43,350,

which covered the repayment of a grant the council had received in support of their aborted plans for the ship in Hebburn. The purchase was formally completed on 23 December 1998. As part of the deal, the trust agreed to remove *Cavalier* from the dry dock by 31 May 1999, thereby enabling Cammell Laird (Tyneside) to complete its purchase of the former Hawthorn Leslie Shipyard from the council and reopen it for commercial repairs.

Before that could happen, Cammell Laird carried out a package of repairs including the removal of asbestos, blasting back several sections of the ship to bare metal, replacing a lot of metalwork, especially along the waterline, completely repainting the ship's exterior and ballasting her for the tow. On completion of the work, the semi-derelict machinery for the dock gate had to be coaxed into action to release *Cavalier* into the Tyne for the 300-mile tow down the east coast to Chatham, where she received a tremendous welcome on 16 May 1999 and was temporarily placed within No 3 basin. Three days later, she entered No 2 dry dock, the site of the old single dock where Lord Nelson's flagship HMS *Victory* was built. Tours of the upper decks began soon after her arrival, while the Historic Dockyard's employed conservation team and dedicated volunteers started work to enable more parts of the ship to be opened to the public. Visitors were finally allowed down below in August 2001, following the completion of the forward mess deck's restoration.

Cavalier now forms part of a three-ship line-up in the heart of the Historic Dockyard at Chatham, the trio consisting of sloop *Gannet*, the Submarine *Ocelot* and *Cavalier*. (*Chatham Historic Dockyard Trust*)

7 | THE NATIONAL DESTROYER MEMORIAL

HMS CAVALIER

HAVING SECURED *CAVALIER*'S SURVIVAL, THE
trust could also begin fulfilling its other founding
objective by starting work on a suitable memorial to
those who lost their lives in the Royal Navy's destroyers
in the Second World War. To ensure that this sensitive
project gained the full support of the veterans and
their families, the trust invited the Dean of Rochester,
the Very Reverend Edward Shotter, to act as the
chairman of an independent memorial steering
committee. Its members consisted of representatives
from a wide range of interested bodies, including the
Royal Navy, Royal Naval Association, 8th Destroyer
Association, Royal British Legion, HMS *Cavalier*
Association and The Friends of HMS *Cavalier* Trust. The
committee solicited views from anyone with an interest
in the subject and sent out some 17,000 papers during
the comprehensive public consultation process, to
request comments about the memorial's form, content
and location. The replies were incorporated within the
design brief that formed the basis of a call for expres-
sions of interest from artists, which was issued via the
Kent Architecture Centre. An evaluation of the thirty-
six applicants by the architecture centre and the
steering group managed to whittle the group down to
a short list of six artists who were asked to prepare
outline proposals and two, Kate Denton and Kenneth
Potts, were commissioned to develop their concepts to
model stage. On 5 March 2004, the trust announced

Another party of school children are given the opportunity to gain an insight into the lives of those who served in the Royal Navy's wartime destroyers during a guided tour of Cavalier.

that Kenneth Potts had been chosen to produce the
memorial. The acclaimed sculptor had been a designer
for Royal Worcester before specialising in bronze
portraits and had recently completed a statue of Air
Vice Marshal 'Johnnie' Johnson.

By 2007 he had created a substantial piece of public
art with a length of 12ft 6in and a height of 10ft 6in
mounted on a granite plinth of recycled dock stone
beside HMS *Cavalier*. One side of the memorial is
dominated by a list of the 142 Royal Navy destroyers
lost in the Second World War, together with a formal
acknowledgement of the sacrifice of the other British
Dominion and Allied destroyers that were sunk
between 1939 and 1945. The other side is a dramatic
bronze relief which captures the courage of the men
who served in the wartime destroyers, along with the
combined threats they faced on a daily basis from a
hostile environment and a ruthless enemy. Describing
what he was trying to achieve, Kenneth Potts said at
the time, 'My design concept centres on a destroyer in
action, with a graphic depiction of the lives of the men
who served in her. HMS *Cavalier* on display at The
Historic Dockyard is inspirational. Yet I was conscious of
the fact that although the ship is afloat, she is in a dry
dock and therefore removed from the two elements

that gave her life, the men and the sea. I have tried to incorporate both and to convey the spirit of the ship in action. The scene is set during an imaginary action on convoy protection duty. The ship is engaged in rescuing survivors from a ship sunk by enemy action, a hazardous procedure that could result in the rescuer becoming a victim of torpedo attack. Beyond the destroyer an expanse of sea graphically portrays the harsh environment of the Atlantic and Arctic wastes in which the convoys operated. The gunners are training their guns on a U-Boat.'

HRH The Duke of Edinburgh, who served in the destroyers *Whelp* and *Chequers*, agreed to unveil the memorial. He suggested that if the event was held within a few days of Remembrance Sunday, the Navy could assist by sending the 96-strong Naval Guard, which had been formed to participate within the national commemorations at the Cenotaph, before the sailors returned to their normal duties. Thus His Royal Highness unveiled the memorial on 14 November 2007 during the dedication ceremony led by the Chaplain of the Fleet, The Venerable John Green, and the Dean Emeritus of Rochester, The Very Reverend Edward Shotter. The event was also attended by the Band of HM Royal Marines Britannia Royal Naval College, the ship's company of HMS *Ledbury* and 900 guests, including 400 veterans who served in the Navy's wartime destroyers.

At the time of writing, fifteen years have passed since *Cavalier* returned to Chatham. As will be seen in the remainder of this book, *Cavalier's* overall condition has been transformed by the hard work of the Historic Dockyard's dedicated band of volunteers and three employed members of staff who also care for HM Submarine *Ocelot* and HMS *Gannet*. Thanks to their combined efforts, *Cavalier's* future seems assured for many years to come.

Top, right: Visitors to *Cavalier* are greeted by the memorial's dramatic bronze relief. It captures the courage of the men who served in the wartime destroyers, along with the combined threats they faced on a daily basis from a hostile environment and a ruthless enemy.

Far right: Close up views of the memorial's dramatic bronze relief.

Opposite: The other side of the memorial contains a list of the 142 Royal Navy destroyers lost in the Second World War, together with a formal acknowledgement of the sacrifice of the other British Dominion and Allied destroyers that were sunk between 1939 and 1945.

Right: HRH The Duke of Edinburgh unveils the National Destroyer Memorial alongside *Cavalier* on 14 November 2007. (*Chatham Historic Dockyard Trust*)

Above, right: The memorial's dedication by the Duke of Edinburgh was recorded for posterity by this plaque.

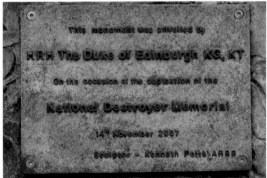

THE HULL

Cavalier's hull represents an important transitional phase in the development of twentieth-century warship construction, being built to a hybrid method that incorporated the use of traditional riveting and modern welding techniques.

CAVALIER'S PRINCIPAL STATISTICS
on completion were as follows:

Length Overall 362ft 9in
Length Between Perpendiculars 339ft 6in
Beam 35ft 9in
Displacement
    1,781 tons (light condition)
    2,202 tons (half oil)
    2,510 tons (deep)
Draught
Maximum Forward 12ft 6in
Maximum Aft 15ft 11in
Machinery
    2 X Admiralty 3-drum boiler, twin shafts, Parsons
    single reduction geared turbines producing a
    combined output of 40,000 SHP
Speed 32 knots
Range
    1,450 miles @ 31 knots (maximum sea speed)
    3,900 miles @ 20 knots
    5,500 miles @ 15 knots
Complement 225 officers and ratings

Left: Cavalier carried a single stockless anchor either side of the bow. The port side one is seen here, secured within the hawsepipe.

Below: The contrast in appearance between the smooth finish of *Cavalier*'s welded bow and the lines of rivets that were used to secure the majority of the hull's metal plates is clearly evident.

Bottom: The raised fo'c'sle became a distinctive characteristic of the destroyers that were built for the Royal Navy in the first half of the twentieth century.

Below, right: *Cavalier*'s hull incorporates a number of changes that were introduced to the standard war production destroyer's hull design before the Admiralty placed orders for the 3rd Emergency Flotilla. These included the incorporation of a transom stern to improve the performance at higher speeds.

Right: The hatch situated between the two scuttles is an escape hatch. 6in Roman numerals can be seen below the hatch which indicate the ship's draught towards the stern. On some ships they would have been cut in by chisel or centre punch, whereas metal figures were used for this purpose on *Cavalier*'s hull. This image shows that *Cavalier* currently draws 10ft aft.

Far right: A close-up view of the riveted construction used to secure the majority of the hull's steel plates to each other and to the main structural members.

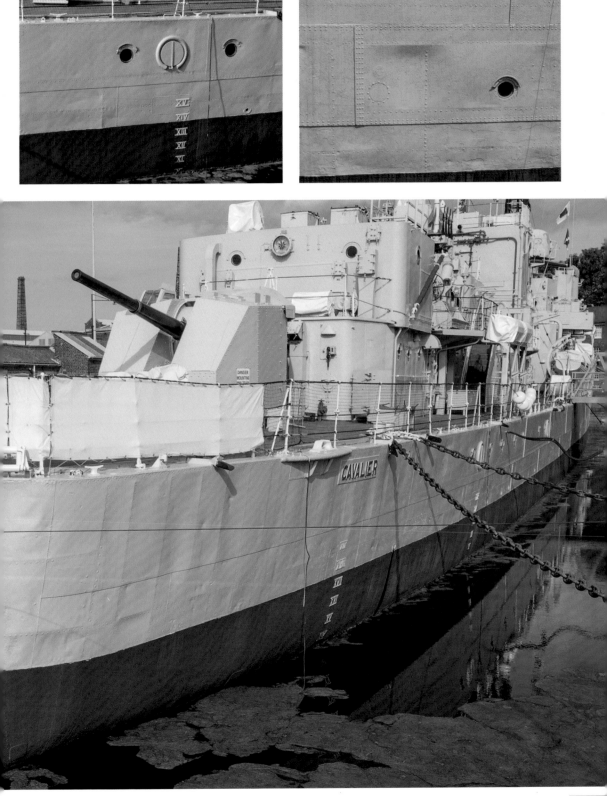

THE FO'C'SLE & FORWARD 4.5in GUNS

The ship's anchor cables and shore lines were handled on the fo'c'sle, while the forward set of 4.5in guns formed part of *Cavalier*'s main armament.

Below: Normally, the Union Flag can only be used as a jack by HM ships in commission and forms part of a suit of colours. Strictly speaking, this suit consists of the White Ensign, the Union Flag and the masthead pennant or the distinguishing flag of an embarked flag officer. However, the term 'colours' usually refers to just the ensign and jack. The jack is worn during designated daylight hours by HM ships while they are at anchor, secured to a buoy or berthed alongside. The only two occasions it is worn by a ship underway is when she is wearing the Royal Standard or escorting a ship in which the Sovereign is embarked, or while underway in a harbour when the other stationary ships are dressed overall. In a bid to maintain as much of the destroyer's naval character as possible, the HMS *Cavalier* Trust secured permission for the Union Flag to be worn as a jack.

Below right: The term forecastle, always pronounced fo'c'sle, dates back to the Middle Ages, when fighting ships were fitted with a raised structure over the bows and stern. Armed men would be stationed in these 'castles' to repulse boarders or attack the men on enemy ships. The term is now used to describe the forward section of the upper deck where the anchor cables and shore lines are handled. In this elevated view of *Cavalier's* fo'c'sle, the route taken by the two anchor cables can be clearly seen. Each one runs up through its respective hawsepipe to a combined capstan and cable holder, before it descends below the deck through a navel pipe to the cable locker in the forepeak. Today, *Cavalier* is held in the middle of No 2 dock by chain cables secured to bollards on the fo'c'sle and the side of the dock.

The dock itself is a significant historical artefact in its own right. Its origins date back to the building of the shallow,

timber-lined Old Single Dock in 1623 which was used for the construction of Nelson's flagship HMS *Victory* between 23 July 1759 and 7 May 1765. The Old Single Dock was subsequently rebuilt in stone and extended from 1855 to 1856. Four years later, it was used for the construction of HMS *Achilles*, the first iron-hulled warship to be built in a Royal Dockyard. To mark the bicentenary of Trafalgar and its links to Nelson's flagship, the then Second Sea Lord, Vice Admiral Sir James Burnell-Nugent, formally renamed it the Victory Dock during a ceremony on 23 July 2005.

Right: A close-up of the bullring on the stem-head through which bridles would have been led back when making fast to a buoy.

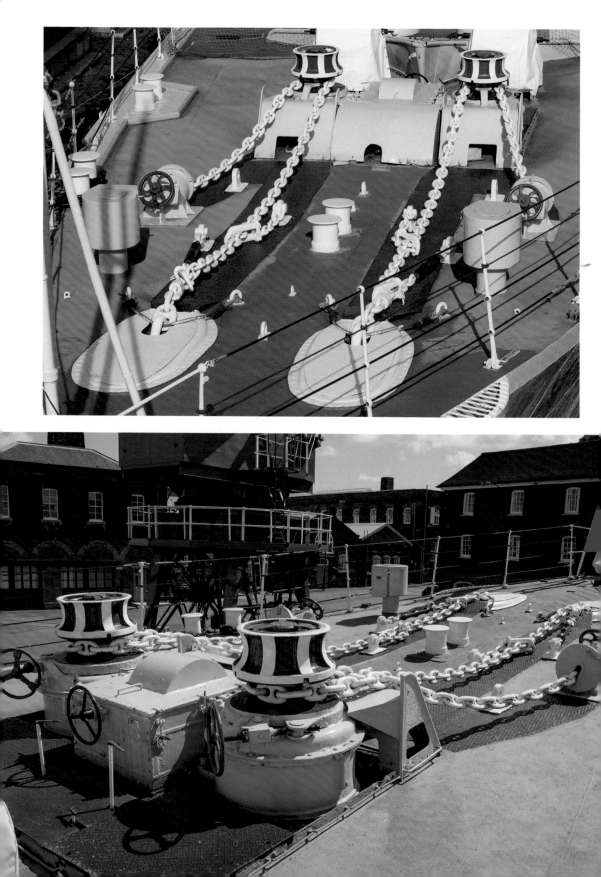

Opposite, above and below: Good views looking fore and aft, showing the overall arrangements for handling the two anchor cables.

Above: The steam-driven combined capstans and cable holders for the port and starboard anchor cables.

Above: The hand-operated wheel, mounted astern of the combined capstan and cable holder, controlled the brake, which governed the speed of the anchor cable when letting go of an anchor or while hauling it back in.

Below: A screw slip has been attached to the port anchor cable to heave the anchor close home in its hawsepipe and would have always been used when the ship was secured for sea. The metal fitting attached to the anchor cable at the bottom of the photo is part of the brake slip which could be used to hold the cable temporarily while handing the inboard end of the cable.

Below: The port bonnet is fitted with a compressor. When screwed down it would nip a link of cable.

Bottom: A watertight ready-use shell locker for A mounting situated immediately aft of the breakwater.

4.5in QF Mk IV GUNS

ON COMPLETION, *CAVALIER* WAS ARMED with four single 4.5in Quick Firing Mk IV guns capable of engaging attacking aircraft or hitting targets up to 10 miles away. They were ballistically identical to the earlier marks of this gun, but they were modified to suit the CP Mk V mountings which had been developed from the earlier 4.7in CP XXII mountings. Each gun weighs 2.814 tons, including the breech mechanism, and could be elevated to any angle from 10° depression to 55°. The calibre proved to be the optimum for the Royal Navy's destroyers in terms of handling, ballistics and range. The individual mountings fitted to *Cavalier* weigh 12.926 tons including the gun and open-backed shield made of protective plating with a thickness of up to 0.375in. The mountings were identified by a letter: A and B (upper) for those forward of the bridge, X and Y (lower) for those mounted aft. X mounting was removed during *Cavalier*'s modernisation of 1955–57 and the surviving mountings were fitted with Remote Power Control (RPC). From then on they could be trained and elevated automatically at up to 20° per second. It took the gun crews at least 4.3 seconds to load, fire, recoil and reload which meant they could achieve a maximum rate of fourteen rounds per minute.

Right: The metal structure overlapping A mounting acted as a shield to protect its gun crew from the blast of B gun when it was fired.

Opposite right: The starboard side of B mounting. The small glazed lookout hood can be clearly seen.

Far right: Whenever the 4.5in guns were not required for use, they were fitted with watertight plugs, known as tompions, which carried a medallion in the form of the ship's badge.

DANGER
MOUNTING
MAY TRAIN
WITHOUT
WARNING

PLEASE TAKE CARE!
WATCH YOUR STEP AND MIND YOUR
HEAD AT ALL TIMES WHEN ONBOARD

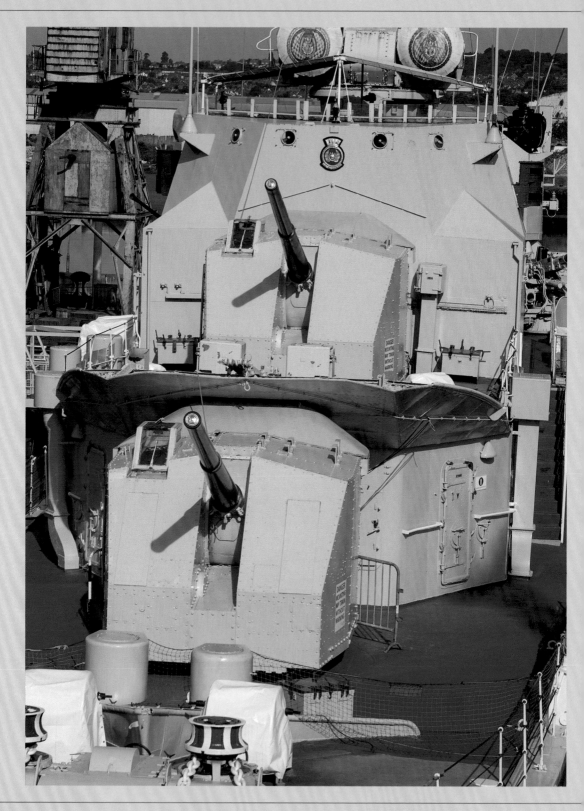

Opposite: This view clearly shows the small gap between the blast shield and the top of A mounting.

Above: B mounting's training position can be clearly seen to the righthand side of the 4.5in gun. It was retained, following the fitting of remote power control during the 1955–57 refit, for standby use in local control.

Right: A close-up view of the elevating position on the lefthand side of the mounting. By using the handles, the guns could be elevated to any angle from 10° depression to 55°.

Below: The gun crews for A and Y mountings manhandled the shells and cartridges from ammunition hand outs in the side of the superstructure to the tray shown in the foreground which was manually moved up in line for loading into the hand-worked breech mechanism.

BELOW DECKS
FORWARD

The forward half of the ship includes messdecks, the main galley, the NAAFI, the ship's office, the bridge wireless office and the transmitting station.

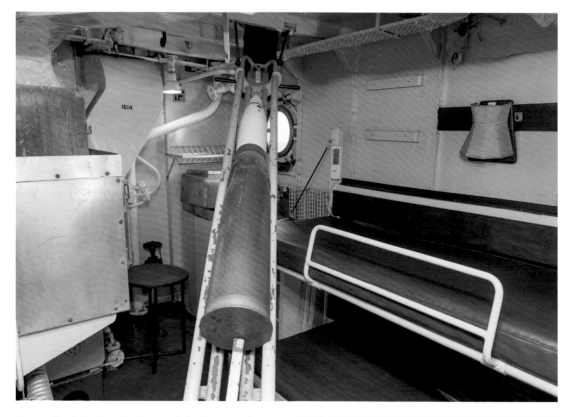

Above: *Cavalier*'s ratings lived, ate, and slept in cramped messes that were squeezed into every available space, including compartments filled with equipment such as this channel which was used to pass the shells and cartridges up to the gun crew of B mounting.

On completion, the destroyer's ratings all slept in hammocks until she underwent her 1964–66 refit in Gibraltar. The limited space in the destroyer ruled out a complete switch to bunks and several ratings still had to use either a camp bed or hammock until she paid off in 1972. This particular mess, situated on 1 deck immediately below B mounting, illustrates why hammocks could not be entirely eliminated in *Cavalier*. It was originally home to twelve petty officers until the switch to bunks, when the number that could be accommodated dropped to eight. To make the most of the space occupied by the bunks they were mounted in up to three tiers wherever possible. In these tight confines ratings needed a mixture of friendliness, cheerfulness, discipline and a good sense of humour. To help pass the time whilst off duty, they frequently organised competitions in their messdecks for various card and board games including 'uckers' (Ludo), crib, draughts and chess.

Right: This round of 4.5in ammunition has been cut in half to provide visitors with an idea of its contents. Measuring just over 4ft in length, a complete round consisted of a fuze at the top, a shell and then a brass cartridge. The cordite propellant accounted for 11lb of the brass cartridge's total weight of 38½lb and was packed around the black electric primer. The high effect (HE) shells weighed 55lb and were fitted with variable-time (VT) fuses for anti-aircraft use. *Cavalier* also carried semi armour-piercing (SAP), practice and star shells.

Right: The hinged solid metal plate, known as the deadlight, could be secured across the scuttle and was used either to preserve its watertight integrity in the event of the glass being broken, or to assist the darkening of the ship when required. In hot climates, wind scoops were fitted to the outside of the scuttles to assist the air circulation through the living spaces.

Below right: The space occupied by the bunks was also used for recreation. To achieve this the middle bunk could be folded back to transform the two lower bunks into a settee for use when the sailors were off duty. Afterwards, folding tables were brought out to provide a suitable surface for eating meals or for games, ash trays, drinks, etc when the sailors were relaxing. All of the food was cooked centrally in the main galley. The senior hand of the mess organised a daily roster to nominate one rating to act as cook of the mess. The chosen sailor collected the meals from the galley and served out the food. To cope with the less than ideal method of distribution, the food was generally stodgy and unimaginative, although rarely in short supply. After each meal, the designated sailor would clean up and return all of the dishes and utensils that had been borrowed from the galley. The remaining cutlery and crockery was kept in lockers in the messdeck. Some of the cook's other duties including collecting the rum issue unless the messdeck had a designated Rum Bo's'n, making the stand-easy tea and replenishing the messdeck's supply of tea, sugar and milk from the stores.

Below: This wooden board recorded the whereabouts of the ship's senior officers whenever she was alongside, anchored or secured to a buoy.

Bottom right: This is one of two ammunition hoists within the petty officer's mess. Situated on the port side, this one brought up the cartridges for the 4.5in gun from the magazine while the hoist on the starboard side brought up the shells.

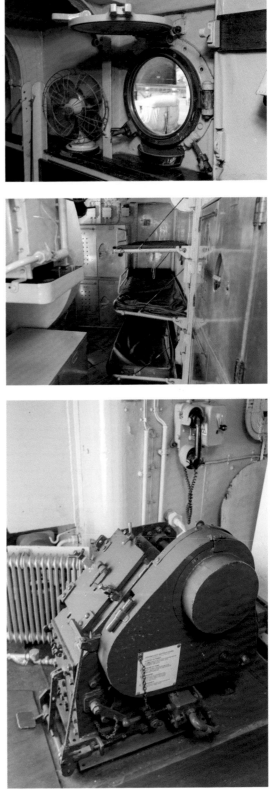

Above: One of forward messdecks on the port side of 2 deck. The aluminium kit lockers, either side of the watertight door, contained each person's belongings while the space above was used to store their suitcases.

Left: Most messdecks had an electric toaster.

Bottom: One of the watertight hatches leading to the messdeck below.

Opposite top: The cut-down wooden cask, known as a grog-tub or scuttlebutt, is a reminder of a cherished naval tradition that was observed in *Cavalier* for most of her time in commission. Until its abolition on 31 July 1970 every rating over the age of 20 was entitled to receive one tot (one eighth of a pint) of rum each day, or given a cash allowance. The practice began in 1687 when the Royal Navy introduced a daily issue of rum in place of brandy. Men were entitled to one pint of neat rum per day, while boys were given half a pint. In 1740 Admiral Edward Vernon, universally known as 'Old Grog' due to the grogram boat cloak he always wore, tried to reduce the amount of drunkenness in the Fleet by ordering the ration to be watered down with two parts water to one part rum, and splitting the daily issue into two halves. The first half was to be administered at noon, followed by the other half at 1800. He also directed that the rum should be distributed to the tune of Nancy Dawson from a cut-down cask embellished with 'God Save the King' (or Queen) in brass letters. This watered down drink swiftly became known as grog. Subsequent orders reduced the amount of rum that was issued, as well as the number of qualifying personnel. However, it remained one of the Royal Navy's most valued

privileges. Chief petty officers and petty officers were issued with neat rum. To give an idea of the amount of rum that was consumed in *Cavalier*, it was estimated that ratings drank 56,064 tots during the 18-month-long second commission.

Right: One of the emergency lanterns that were strategically located between decks to illuminate important spaces or gangways in the event of the main lighting system's failure.

Far right: A gentle reminder that each sailor's daily tot of rum was for their personal consumption only. Even though sailors were forbidden to hoard their tot or give it to other sailors, it was used illegally by some to secure favours such as swapping duties or to arrange for the slinging of their hammock after evening rounds while they were ashore on leave.

A rating died recently because he had drunk an excessive amount of

RUM

Well-meaning "FRIENDS" had pressed him to have "SIPPERS" and "GULPERS" on his

BIRTHDAY

THIS FORM OF HOSPITALITY, WITH ITS TRAGIC CONSEQUENCES, IS AGAINST THE REGULATIONS

Left: This manhole leads down to the ASDIC compartment on 4 deck.

Below: At the time of *Cavalier's* completion, the Royal Navy referred to sonar as ASDIC after the Anti-submarine Detection/ Indication Committee which was set up as an Anglo-French project in 1918. The director of the Harvard Under Water Sound Laboratory during WWII, F V (Ted) Hunt, came up with the term sonar in 1942 as a phonetic analogue to radar which was already in widespread use in America. When thinking of a potentially suitable word to describe 'sound radar' he initially thought of sodar before settling on the term sonar. To justify its use as a credible acronym, Hunt subsequently defined sonar as standing for Sounding Navigation and Ranging. The introduction of the term sonar to the Royal Navy's vocabulary did not occur as swiftly as the transition from RDF to radar. When the idea was originally mooted in 1944 it encountered strong opposition from a number of senior officers involved in anti-submarine warfare. They felt that the term ASDIC represented the pioneering work of those who had been involved in this field of development during the interwar years and its retention would help inspire those who were going to build on their achievements in the coming years. Despite the resistance to this change, the Royal Navy finally succumbed to American pressure by adopting the term sonar in the early 1950s.

Below left & bottom right: *Cavalier* was originally fitted with Type 144 ASDIC which had a search capability out to 3,000 yards. Designed to work with ahead thrown weapons, principally the hedgehog, it was the first attempt to create an integrated anti-submarine weapon system that incorporated an amount of automation, thereby representing a step change

in the development of ASDIC. The Type 144 had a Q attachment fitted below the main retractable transducer which emitted a narrow, vertical, wedge-shaped beam approximately 3° wide in the horizontal plane. It extended the coverage of the ASDIC's main beam to an angle of 60° in the vertical plane which enabled contact to be maintained with a submarine at a range of 1,500 yards to a depth of between 300ft and 700ft. The Type 144 was replaced during the 1955–57 refit by the retractable Type 164 sonar. Its improved features included the new listening set, Type 174, along with enhanced bearing and range recorders capable of detecting targets to a depth of 1,500ft. The latter incorporated a pair of additional plotting scales, 0–1,500 yards for attack and 0–3,000 yards for searching only. The retractable transducer's hydraulic lifting/lowering gear can be seen here along with the top of the watertight enclosure in which it is mounted. In contrast to other parts of the ship, this area did not suffer any real deterioration while she was on the Tyne. However, the lower half of the Type 164's dome did not escape unscathed and was crudely hacked away to expose the transducer. The exposed underwater section was subsequently plated in as part of the preparations for the tow to Chatham.

Right: The hull's metal frames and stringers can be clearly seen beside the enclosure for the Type 164 sonar.

Below left & right: The Q beam was replaced by a separate Type 147 sonar during *Cavalier's* modernisation of 1955–57. The new sonar transmitted a fan-shaped beam 3° deep in the vertical plane and 65° wide in the horizontal plane from a retractable streamlined sword-shaped transducer that was mounted ahead of the Type 164 sonar.

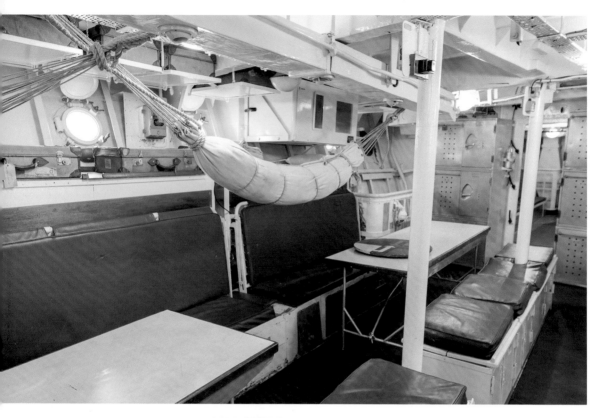

Above: Hammocks were slung just 18in apart and were slung from the overhead metal hooks, known as hammock hooks, that were mounted on brackets or bars placed near the deckhead or on the bulkheads. In the morning, sailors were required to lash up their hammocks and place them in a large open top metal cages known as hammock nettings. When circumstances permitted, they would be aired up on deck. Hammocks were never shared and were primarily used as a sailor's personal, portable, compact bed. If the hammock's owner died and had to be buried at sea, it would become his coffin.

Left: The lamp and paint store continues to be used for its original purpose and accommodates some of the paint that is required for her ongoing maintenance. During *Cavalier*'s final commission, 1,032 brushes were used to apply 730 gallons of grey paint and 420 gallons of deck paint.

Bottom left: Some of the hammocks were stored during the day in this open topped metal cage which was referred to as a hammock netting. In the event of an emergency they could be used by a damage control party to plug holes in the side of the hull until a more effective solution could be implemented.

Opposite: Running from the forward messdecks to the main galley, this passageway, on the port side of 2 deck, was officially known as the port passage and unofficially referred to as the 'Burma Way'. It provided access to a number of compartments including the ship's office, the NAAFI, the bridge wireless office, and the TS annexe.

Above: Manned by a petty officer and leading writer, the ship's office was the smallest sub-department of the supply and secretariat division. Despite the team's modest size, it dealt with all of the pay and correspondence.

Above: The Navy Army and Air Force Institute's (NAAFI) canteen. The ship's company could buy a wide selection of items from this shop including duty-free tobacco, toothpaste, writing paper, and shoe polish. A percentage of the profits that were made by the NAAFI were ploughed back into the canteen fund, which was managed by a committee and could be spent on items to improve the welfare of the ship's company as a whole.

Below: The perspex-domed Gyro Rate Unit Stabiliser (GRUS) Mk 4, located within the unmanned TS annexe, was used to stabilise the Mk 6M DCT against the ship's motion and act as a reference to calculate rates for airborne targets.

Above: All of the ship's radio receivers and some of the transmitters were located within the bridge wireless office.

Below and right: The heads. This name was originally given to the area forward of the fo'c'sle that was used as the seamen's lavatory. The term was always used in the plural to indicate the weather and lee sides – the sailors were expected to use the lee side to ensure everything fell clear into the sea. The term continues to be used by sailors to describe these facilities, even though they are now fitted within a ship's hull. The cleaner of the heads was known as the 'captain of the heads'.

THE MAIN GALLEY

SITUATED BELOW THE MAINMAST, THIS WAS the main galley for the ship's company. During her final two years in commission it was estimated that the ship's company ate 16,000 yards of sausages, 130 tons of potatoes, 30,000,000 square inches of bread, 24,300,000 individual baked beans, 180,000 eggs, and drank half a million cups of tea. A further two galleys were located within the aft superstructure and brought into use whenever it was too dangerous for the men to reach the main galley in rough weather. The cramped conditions within *Cavalier* ruled out the possibility of introducing centralised messing whereby the ship's company ate their meals in a dedicated dining hall. With the notable exception of the officers, the ship's company continued to eat in their messdecks until she paid off in 1972.

Top: Once the food had been cooked, a designated member of each mess collected the meals on behalf of his fellow sailors from this serving counter.

Top: The ship's cooks had to work in cramped conditions as they prepared approximately 200 meals for the entire ship's company.

Above: The boiling coppers.

Right: Catering on this scale required scaled-up versions of the type of equipment found in the average household's kitchen, such as this mixer.

Middle left: The food preparation surfaces can be seen to the right.

Left: The upper oven.

The radar warning office is one of the areas to have benefited from the vision of those serving in the ship who began the campaign to save *Cavalier* before she paid off for the last time in July 1972. As a direct result of their actions, the subsequent de-storing process was restricted to the removal of the most sensitive items of equipment until her ultimate fate had been determined. Without this foresight, the radar warning office would have been gutted and probably taken many years to re-equip. This compartment contained all of the transmitters and receivers associated with the ship's surface radar systems. By today's standards these items of equipment are incredibly bulky yet in the 1950s they would have been viewed as leading-edge technology.

Left: Part of the Identification Friend or Foe (IFF) equipment controlling the Type 944 interrogator which was co-ordinated with the Type 293Q Radar.

Bottom left: Part of the Identification Friend or Foe (IFF) equipment for the Type 954 IFF Mk X.

Below: Test equipment for the Type 293Q consisting of the wavemeter, standing wave ratio indicator and spectrometer.

Bottom right: The transmitter and modulator unit for the Type 293Q.

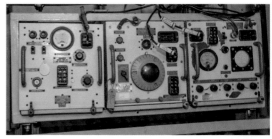

Above: The radar warning office's equipment included the modulator, transmitter and receiver panels for the Type 293Q radar. The display unit and the control unit for the Type 293Q's distinctive 'cheese' aerial can be seen here. These were not normally used for operational purposes, but could be used as an emergency operating position if required.

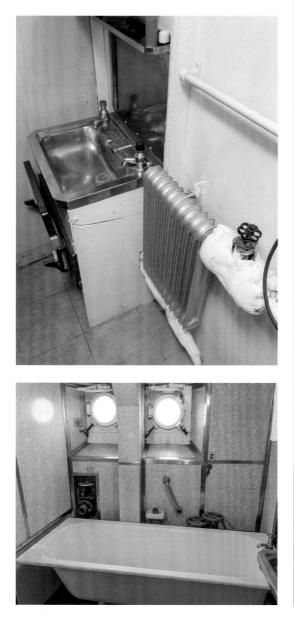

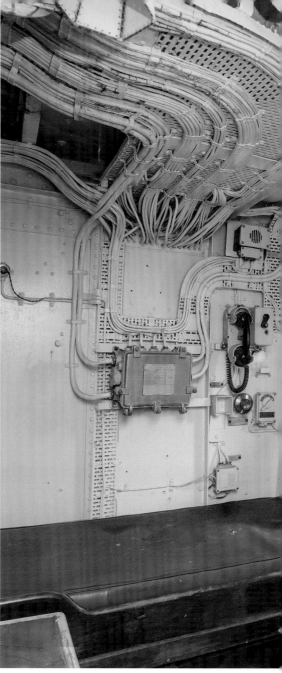

Top: The radiator and stainless steel wash basin in the marine engineering officer's cabin.

Above: The officers' bathroom.

Above: The cables running along the deck head of the marine engineering officer's cabin illustrate the dramatic increase in the amount of electrical equipment fitted during *Cavalier*'s time in commission. The air-conditioning unit mounted above the scuttle helped improve the quality of life onboard during the ship's deployments to the Far East. Some of the units were fitted rather crudely to the cabins used by junior officers. They were fitted flush against the side of the hull within an opening that had been cut in the bulkhead, so that one half of the fan produced cold air for one cabin, while the other half catered for the second cabin.

Above: The passageway on the starboard side of 2 deck which leads to the transmitting station. The watertight hatch in the foreground leads down to five cabins that would have been used by officers and are closed to the public. Although visitors have unrestricted access to several parts of the ship, a small number of compartments, including the transmitting station, have discreet barriers across their entrance to either prevent souvenir hunters from acquiring the smaller items on display, or to protect visitors from potential hazards within a specific compartment.

Right: A close up view of the 'tallboy' console's microphone within the transmitting station.

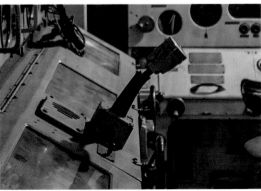

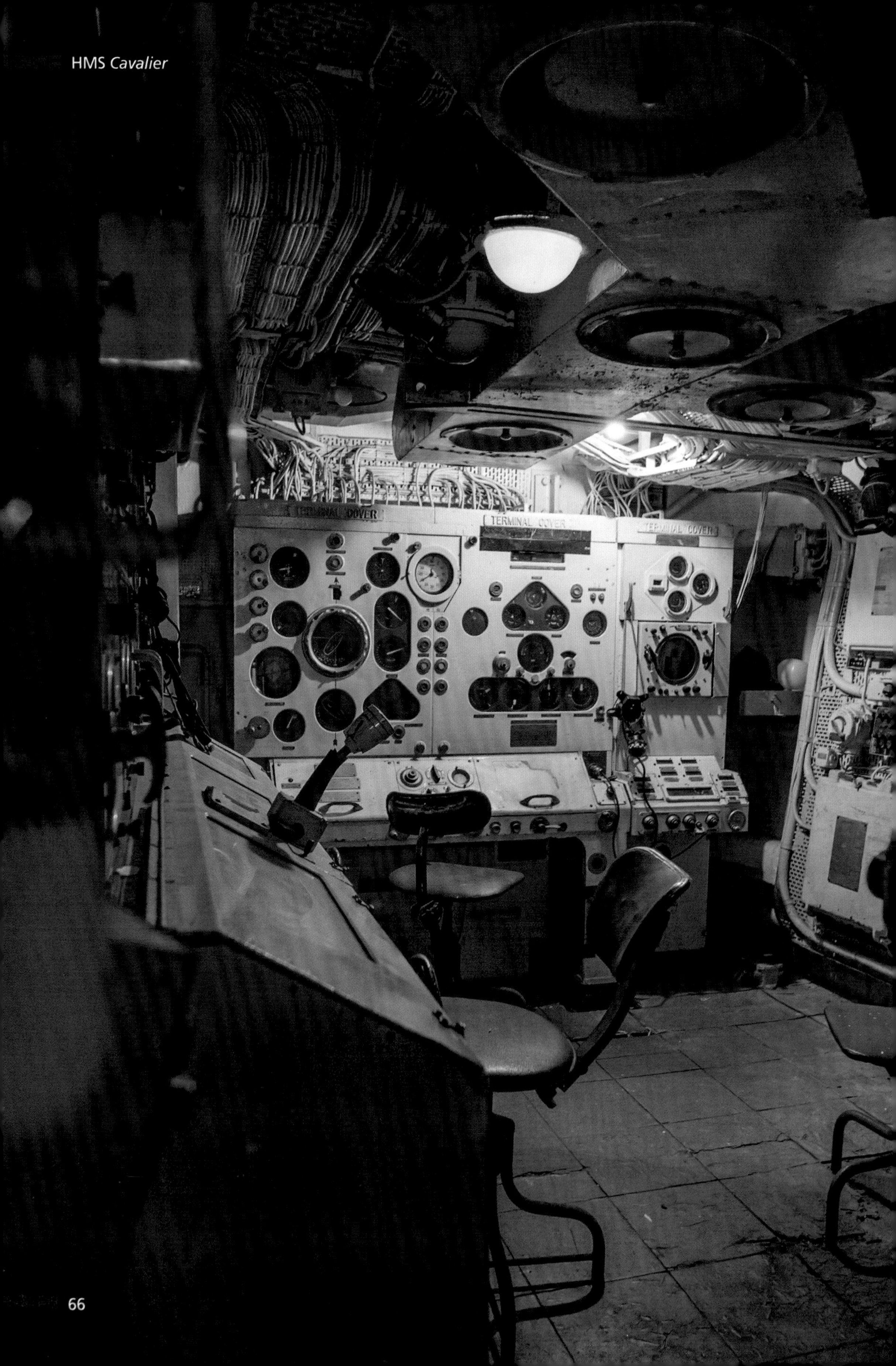
TERMINAL COVER

Left: The term transmitting station was used to describe the compartment below decks which contained the consoles for target tracking and control equipment for the associated weapons. Manned by three operators, the equipment on the left, known as the 'tallboy' console, was used for blind tracking either air or surface targets using the Mk 6M director's Type 275 radar.

Right: The transmitting station officer's control panel.

Below: The mechanical surface predictor Admiralty Fire Control Box (AFCB) 10 was manned by three operators and used to track, predict and engage surface targets with one or more of the three 4.5in guns. The 'upright piano' format adopted for the AFCB10 resulted in a smaller footprint when compared to the 'table' design used for earlier predictors. Situated in the adjacent TS annexe, the Flyplane 5 electric predictor would be relied on when engaging airborne targets.

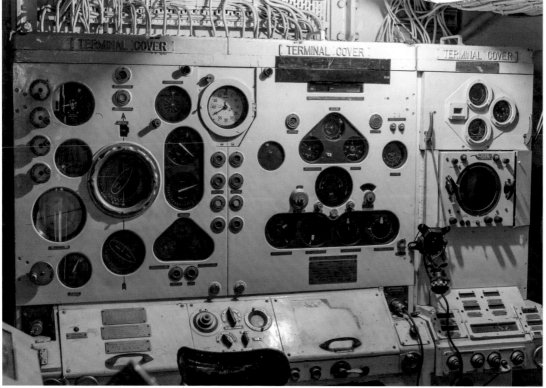

THE FORWARD SUPER-STRUCTURE

The fitting of *Cavalier's* current bridge was one of the most extensive alterations to be carried out during her modernisation of 1955–57. Based on the design of the bridge created for the *Daring* class it is perceived as the ship's nerve centre with its combination of the compass platform, operations room, flag deck and Mk 6M director.

CAVALIER WAS AMONG THE FIRST FOUR SHIPS of the CA class to be modernised and she received a new bridge modelled on the distinctive one designed for the *Daring* class, rather than the ungainly looking frigate-type enclosed bridge added to the second quartet to be modernised.

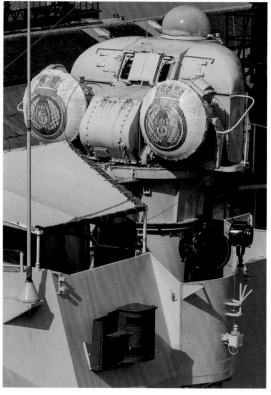

Above: The forward superstructure's boxy design at 01 deck level created the largest possible internal volume for the new operations room. The distinctive angled profile adopted for the deck above offset the slab-sided appearance of the boxy lower level to create a pleasing, purposeful-looking bridge.

Right: The lights may have gone, but the housing for the port side navigation light remains on the side of the bridge.

Opposite: The steps leading down from the narrow side deck, linking the flag deck and the short deck on which B mounting is situated, were fitted in Portsmouth Dockyard immediately before the Ministry of Defence handed over the destroyer to the HMS *Cavalier* Trust in 1977.

Above left: With no side deck between the 40mm Bofors and B mounting, the starboard side of the forward superstructure has a rather slab-sided appearance in contrast to the port side.

Above: The curved steel work softened the inevitable step between the raised fo'c'sle and 2 deck, which became a distinctive feature of the destroyers built for the Royal Navy in the first half of the twentieth century.

Left: The biggest reproduction of the ship's badge is attached to the forward face of the bridge. Cast in bronze, it weighs approximately 12kg. Gold leaf was used to achieve a long-lasting finish capable of withstanding the rigours of the marine environment. The design for the ship's official badge incorporated elements from the Coat of Arms used by Charles I's nephew, Prince Rupert of the Rhine, who commanded the royalist (Cavalier) cavalry during the English Civil War. These included the chequered pattern, lion and coronet, while the horseshoe and wings refer to the cavalry.

Right: Two circular Kent clear view screens can be seen in the forward part of the bridge. They were originally developed in the 1930s for the car industry as an alternative to conventional windscreen wipers. However, it quickly became apparent that they were better suited to the marine environment and can be found on a wide cross-section of vessels from small motor boats to ships, including *Cavalier* which has a total of four in the front of her bridge. The electric motor in the middle spins the circular glass at high speed to keep it clear of snow, rain or spray.

THE WARDROOM, WHERE THE ELEVEN OFFICERS
would eat their meals and spend their time off duty.
The name evolved from the term wardrobe room and,
strictly speaking, refers to the space in which the
officers eat their meals. On larger warships there is
usually a separate relaxation area known as the
wardroom ante room. However, there was no room for
such luxuries in *Cavalier*. The president of the
wardroom mess was normally the executive officer. The
captain would be offered honorary membership and
only enter the wardroom by invitation.

Above: The Historic Dockyard has the ability to recreate how
the wardroom's dining table would have looked when it was
laid for a meal, thanks to a generous gift from Gillian Wettern.
Her late husband, the author and naval correspondent of *The
Daily Telegraph*, Desmond Wettern, amassed a collection of
china that was used by the Royal Navy in the post war period
during his writing career and service as an officer in the Royal
Naval Reserve. The collection comprises both porcelain and
china, bearing the traditional 'foul anchor' motif and includes
serving platters, coffee pots, plates, cups and saucers.

Right: The officers would keep their napkins in this wooden
holder beside the light switches in the wardroom.

Bottom: The wardroom and captain's pantry situated between
the captain's day cabin and the wardroom. The food would be
prepared in the main galley and brought here before it was
served.

Above: Once the food was ready to be served it would be passed through the serving hatch in the bulkhead and brought from the sideboard to the dining table by one of the stewards. Between meals, the dinner service, cutlery and glasses were kept within the sideboard.

Below left: The two scuttles in the port and starboard sides of the wardroom provided a reasonable amount of natural light, while the two L-shaped settees, either side of the electric fire, created a homely environment in which the officers could relax while off duty.

Below right: These telephone handsets ensured that the officers could be reached via the intercom if required.

THE CAPTAIN'S DAY CABIN DOUBLED UP AS HIS office and recreational space. He would deal with all of his administration at the desk, while the table would be used for meetings, planning, and as a dining table. The captain would also entertain guests here during official visits to the ship. Despite the Historic Dockyard's policy of keeping barriers to a minimum in *Cavalier*, it has been necessary to fit a number of discreet barriers across the doorways of some compartments.

Above: At meal time, the food would be passed through the serving hatch above the sideboard and brought across to the dining table by a steward. The sideboard's two drawers and cupboards were used to store all of the cutlery and crockery that would be used by the Captain and his guests.

Below, left: The voice pipe and intercom ensured that the captain could be reached immediately whenever he was required.

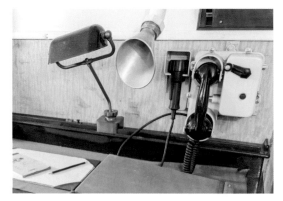

Opposite top: The framed image above the electric fire is a print of *The Laughing Cavalier* by the Dutch artist Frans Hals. The painting acquired its enduring title when it appeared within the Royal Academy's exhibition of 1888, even though the subject is neither a Cavalier nor laughing. Despite these inconvenient facts, the sitter's fine clothing, swagger and jovial appearance matched the public's perception of a typical cavalier's appearance. The painting was subsequently used as the basis for the ship's initial badge. In the absence of an official badge from the Admiralty, it is believed that the first commanding officer, Lieutenant Commander McBarnett, produced the design complete with the motto 'Cavalier's Up'. The Admiralty vetoed the badge and its motto in favour of the current badge with its motto 'Of One Company'.

Opposite bottom: The volunteers finished off their recent restoration of the first lieutenant's cabin by 'dressing' it with a selection of personal items and pieces of uniform to give visitors an idea of how it would have looked when *Cavalier* was in service.

Above & right: The captain was always on call. His cabin was situated a stone's throw away from the ops room and the ladder leading up to the compass platform, which enabled him to reach either area very quickly. Before turning in for the night, whenever the ship was at sea he would leave a set of clear instructions in his night order book for the officer of the watch. These included a summary of expected developments, as well as those circumstances that would require his immediate attention regardless of the hour. If necessary, the captain could be reached immediately via the loudspeaker or voice pipe beside his bunk.

Right: The battle honour boards displayed by many of the Royal Navy's warships record the conflicts in which ships of the same name have participated since the defeat of the Spanish Armada in 1588. For many years warships carried elaborate scrolls, on an unofficial basis, commemorating the significant events that ships of the same name had been involved in. These lists were usually the result of research by a member of the ship's company and sometimes included events that were not subsequently recognised as official battle honours. The Royal Navy finally introduced a formal system to regulate the approval and use of battle honours on 1 October 1954 via Admiralty Fleet Order 2565. Its primary objectives were to foster an *esprit de corps* and encourage a greater interest in naval history. Generally, a battle honour is awarded for those actions resulting in the defeat of the enemy, or when the action was inconclusive but well fought and in exceptional cases where outstanding efforts were made against overwhelming odds. Today, the Royal Navy's warships can only display those battle honours that are officially approved by the Ministry of Defence.

In the case of HMS *Cavalier*, she is the Royal Navy's only warship to bear the name and therefore earned the battle honour which is proudly displayed on this wooden board.

Below: The signals room. The ship's daily orders were prepared in the flag deck signal office. As the name suggests, these set out the ship's programme for the day ahead and would normally be issued on the afternoon of the day before they were due to be carried out. The orders included the names of officers and men detailed to carry out routine duties, any orders or instructions required for duties that differed from the usual routine, and night leave. Every member of the ship's

company was expected to read the daily orders, and no clemency was shown to those who failed to perform their designated duties because they had not done so.

If any signals had to be copied, they were sent to this office to be reproduced using its Gestetner duplicating machine. As one of the best ventilated compartments in the ship, it was a good environment in which to keep this machine so that the operator was not overcome by the effects of the methylated spirit used in the printing process. The signalman who manned this office was referred to in naval slang as a 'bunting tosser' as he was responsible for the signal flags. His other duties included the operation of the signal projectors to communicate with nearby ships using morse code.

Left: Situated next to the flag deck on 1 deck, the wheelhouse acted as the primary steering point for the ship and the place from which the engine orders were transmitted to the engine room using the combined engine order and revolution telegraphs mounted either side of the traditional wooden ship's wheel. The helmsman received his orders from the officer of the watch via the conning broadcast.

Right: Sadly, the original engraved brass plates that were fitted to both the port and starboard side combined engine order and revolution telegraphs were stolen before *Cavalier* arrived in Chatham. They have been fitted with temporary plywood replacements.

Far right: This brass pointer on top of the pedestal indicated the position of the rudder.

Below left: Moving the traditional wooden ship's wheel operated transmitter rams that pumped hydraulic fluid, consisting of glycerine and distilled water, to and from the receiver rams in the tiller flat. To reduce the chances of a complete failure due to battle damage, the hydraulic system is fitted in duplicate. The brass pointer at the top of the pedestal indicates the rudder's position, while the two brass dials mounted either side enable the helmsman to monitor the pressure in each side of the hydraulic system.

Below: If the conning broadcast system failed, contact could be maintained between the compass platform and the wheelhouse via the voice pipe.

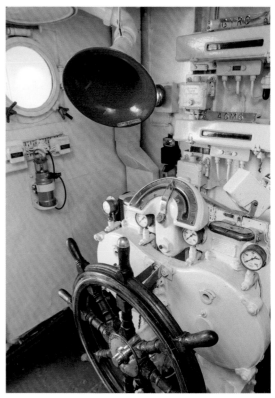

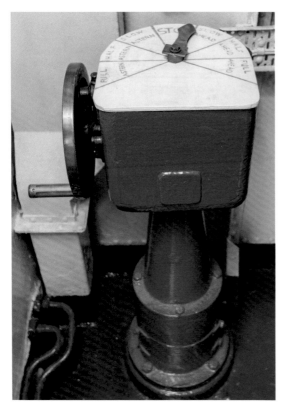

Bellow left: The starboard side combined engine order and revolution telegraph. Alterations to either the engine revolutions or direction could be transmitted to the engine room by turning the appropriate handle on the side of the telegraph. The numerals and brass lever on top of the telegraph displayed the latest settings requested by the officer of the watch on the compass platform.

Below: Whenever the captain, or the officer of the watch, required a change in the rudder's position, it would be displayed on the steering order receiver. The brass bell to the right of the receiver is one of two reply gongs that were used by the engine room to acknowledge a change in engine order. Each gong was differently toned and reserved for one of the two shafts. The standard code for this purpose was: slow, one ring; half, two rings; full, three rings; and stop, two double rings.

THE SINGLE 40mm BOFORS AA GUNS

CAVALIER WAS FITTED WITH A SINGLE 40mm Bofors Mk VII mounting either side of the forward superstructure during the modernisation of 1955–57 as part of her revised close-range armament. It was developed from the twin Mk V Oerilikon mounting of the Second World War and used the same gun as the twin 40mm Bofors Mk V fitted on the aft superstructure during the same refit. Constructed from lightweight alloys, the compact mounting weighed just 1½ tons. It was controlled by the aimer who sat on its port side within a faring that resembled a motorcycle's side-car. He laid and trained the gun using a gyro-gunsight and joystick.

Opposite, above, left: The two elevation counterbalance spring boxes can be seen under the gun barrel in this head-on view of the port side mounting. The open ended tube immediately below the spring boxes is the ejector tube for the spent cartridges.

Above: The open doorway behind the port side mounting's air-cooled gun barrel leads to the wheelhouse, while the closed door behind the white half-height barrier is the entrance to the signals room.

Opposite, left: The port side mounting.

Right: Several clips of deactivated 40mm rounds in the ready-use ammunition 'letter-box' stowages.

Below: The regulator unit for the gyro sight.

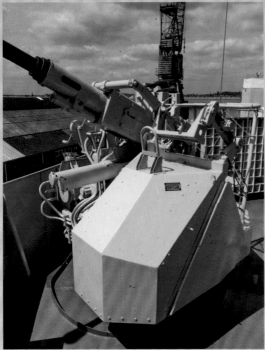

Left: The 40mm gun could be elevated to a maximum angle of 90°.

Below: The hydraulic power unit can be clearly seen above the horizontal pipework. The handles above are the hand-cranks to chain drive the emergency hydraulic pump.

Below: Looking down on the starboard side mounting from the open bridge.

Below: A staghorn bollard and smaller torpedo cleat on the starboard side weather deck.

Below centre: A 50amp switch on the starboard side of the superstructure.

Below right: The external watertight door on the port side of the forward superstructure that leads to the petty officers' mess under B mounting.

Above, left: For maximum efficiency, each individual flag was kept within its own designated 'pigeonhole' inside the signal flag locker at the aft end of the flag deck. When required, the applicable flags were run up the appropriate flag hoist of the fore mast.

Above, right: Looking down from the platform on which the starboard 40mm Bofors is mounted.

Above: The ops room lobby. The large junction boxes underline the huge amount of cabling needed to connect all the equipment within the ops room to their respective sensors.

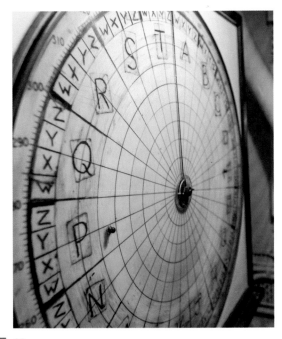

Left: This 'stateboard' mounted by the entrance to the ops room was used to help keep track of the fleet's disposition.

Above: A key element of *Cavalier*'s 1955–57 modernisation was the creation of this ops room immediately below the compass platform, which triggered the reconstruction of the forward superstructure. All the information from the radar, sonar, communications and navigation equipment was collated here. Nicknamed the 'Gloom Room', the ops room was actually quite a pleasant environment in which to work, away from the noise and extreme temperatures endured by those working in other parts of the ship. Air conditioning was essential in this compartment to ensure that the sensitive electronic equipment continued to work, even in the oppressive heat experienced during her time in the Far East Fleet.

In the background is the chart table, with chart storage

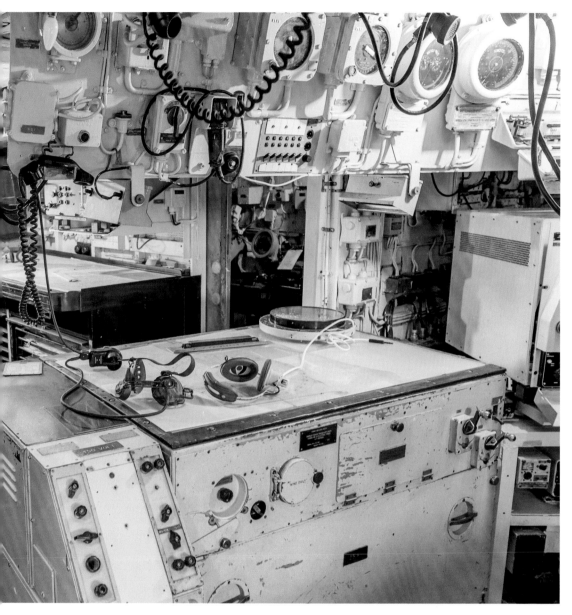

below, where the navigating officer and his assistants plotted the ship's course. The entrance to the ASDIC control room isbe seen ahead of the chart table. This compartment was manned by five men including the first operator who controlled the position of the transducer's detection beam. He estimated the submarine's course and speed from the movement of the echo in the ASDIC beam. The whole team picked up a variety of noises such as whales, porpoises, the sound of other ships' engines and propellers along with the most frightening of all – a torpedo. The JYB automatic plotting table in the foreground maintained an accurate indication of the ship's position.

Right: These displays, connected to the ship's radars, provided continuous updates about potential surface threats. On the right hand side of the image is the table on which the underwater situation was plotted, along with the overhead repeaters.

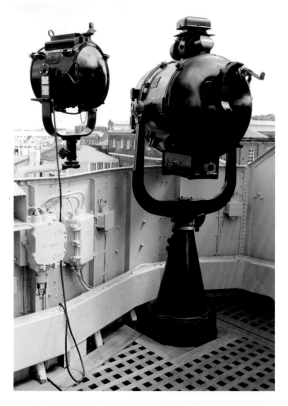

Above & left: The 10in and 20in signal projectors mounted either side at the aft end of the open bridge enabled the signal men to maintain radio silence while communicating with other ships in visual range using Morse code.

Below: This elevated view of the forward superstructure clearly shows the extent of *Cavalier's* open bridge. Today, the awning provides visitors with protection from the elements while they walk round the compass platform and is similar to the one that would have been rigged when *Cavalier* was in service, especially during her time in the Far East.

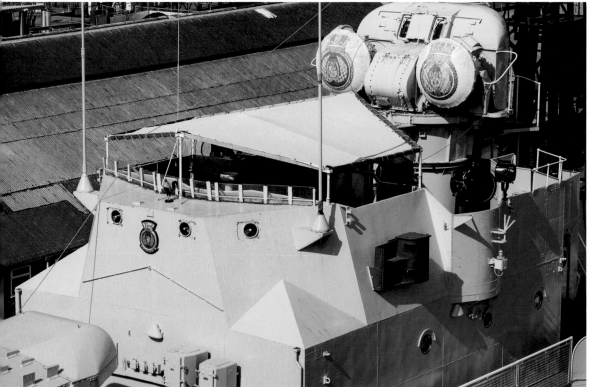

Above & below: The rows of instruments mounted along the inner face of the compass platform's forward bulkhead included the gyro repeater, rudder indicator, engine order and shaft indicator, all of which would have been relied upon by the captain or the officer of the watch while handling the ship.

Above left: The JUA display for the Type 978 high definition warning surface radar that was used mainly for navigation and pilotage.

Above centre: These instruments include the check firing buttons for the 4.5in guns and Seacat missiles.

Above right: The 'stateboard' used to display the underwater situation.

Right: The information displayed by these receivers include the engine revolutions, speed, distance covered, rudder position, and the current course.

Opposite, bottom left: This discreet fitting towards the aft end of the open bridge is a urinal, known as the pig's ear, for the use of the officer of the watch who was unable to leave the compass platform while on watch, even to answer a call of nature.

Right: These glass screens offered some respite from the elements for those on duty on the compass platform.

Below: Sonar bearing display.

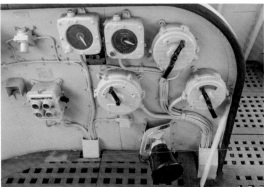

Above: The section of the open bridge aft of the compass platform was known as the gun direction platform. In good visibility, the ship's guns and Seacat missiles could be controlled by the gun direction officer from here. This U-shaped enclosure is dominated by the centre line pelorous sight (T211) which could be used to indicate targets to the Mk 6M director. The sight arm was originally fitted with a pair of binoculars and a pointing stick.

Left: Receivers displaying the target's range and bearing are among the items of equipment mounted on the inner face of the gun direction platform's U-shaped enclosure.

Below: An upper view of the blast shield above A mounting, intended to provide protection to the gun crew when B mounting was fired on an ahead bearing.

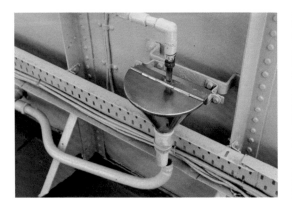

Left: This impressive trophy was presented in February 1972 by Courage Brewery to *Cavalier* to mark her status as 'cock 'o the fleet' following her victory over HMS *Rapid* in 'The Great Race' during the previous summer. A cockerel was a traditional symbol awarded to the winner of Fleet exercises and the brewery's lorries sported a golden cockerel on their roof at the time, so Lieutenant Commander Josh Cosnett managed to persuade the company to present one to the ship. The ship's final commanding officer, Commander P M Goddard, arranged for it to be repainted before the official presentation took place during *Cavalier*'s visit to the Pool of London in July 1972.

Below: The Type 275 gunnery radar's twin antennae could be elevated to a maximum angle of 80°.

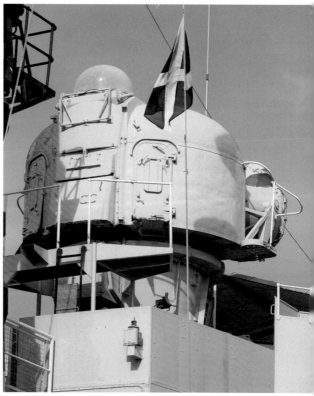

Left: The replacement of the original K Tower Director Control Tower (DCT) and its associated Type 285 radar by the Mk 6M director was an important part of *Cavalier*'s 1955–57 modernisation. The move coincided with the fitting of Remote Power Control (RPC) to the three remaining 4.5in mountings. The director determined the target's range and bearing. This information was fed to the transmitting station for conversion into the required angles of elevation and training for the 4.5in guns which were implemented by remote control.

Above: The Type 275 gunnery radar had two distinctive 'headlamps', one for transmitting, the other for receiving. It could accurately measure the angle of sight which enabled it to be used for blind fire. The ship's badge was painted on the canvas covers for the radar's two 4ft wide dishes to help enhance the destroyer's individual identity.

Right: The 12ft high Mk 6M director achieved valuable weight and manpower savings compared to the earlier Mk VI fitted to the CH-, CO- and CR-class destroyers. The Roman numerals used to identify the previous model betrays its wartime origins while the Arabic numerals of the director fitted to *Cavalier* confirms its status as a post-war system. The improved Mk 6M's three-man crew consisted of a director officer, layer and trainer, in contrast to the seven personnel who were required to man the Mk VI. A reduction in the rotating mass was achieved by fitting the training motors on the fixed structure which, combined with the director's smaller overall size, helped bring the total weight down by 2.2 tons to 9.2 tons. Unlike the Mk IV, it did not have an optical rangefinder, although the director officer could use a sight while looking out of the perspex dome to slew it on to a target.

Above: The fitting of new radars and communication equipment led to a number of modifications to the original lattice fore mast during *Cavalier's* time in commission. The Type AJE aerials are clearly visible at the end of the upper yardarms. They were used for the UHF radios with the aerials on one side used for transmissions while the others were used for receiving. The distinctive semi-circular 'cheese' aerial of the Type 293Q target indication (short-range air search) radar tops the main section of the lattice mast. The sword-like aerial mounted on the end of the yardarm ahead of the Type 293Q was used for intercepting VHF communications.

Left: The smaller radar on the middle platform is the Type 978. This replaced the earlier Type 974 fitted during the modernisation of 1955-57. The Type 974 was a high definition warning surface radar used principally for pilotage and navigation. It could provide high definition of surface targets up to a maximum range of 25 miles. The aerial rotated at a speed of 24 revolutions per minute. Its replacement, the Type 978, was a close range high definition surface warning radar used for pilotage and navigation with an ability to pick up large land masses at a range of 40 miles.

Left: Sadly, only the pedestal antenna of the Type 944 Identification Friend or Foe (IFF) interrogator remains on the fore mast's lowest platform. The Type 944 was a pulsed secondary radar in which a signal transmitted from an interrogator in the ship was received by a transponder fitted in the craft under observation. The transponder would send back an appropriate reply that was picked up by the receiving element of the interrogator.

Below: The top of the fore mast carries the UA-3 electronic surveillance measures (ESM) system. The three quartets of microwave horns were different sizes to cover the following bands (from the top) X, C and S.

AMIDSHIPS

Once home to a pair of quadruple torpedo tubes, the amidships
section includes the machinery spaces, funnel and ship's boats.

Above: The restoration of the funnel is one of the latest projects to be carried out by the conservation team at the Historic Dockyard Chatham. Much of the conservation work is done by the historic warships volunteer group, under the guidance of a full-time ship keeper and his two assistants. The group consists of approximately thirty people, including former servicemen and employees of the dockyard. Their efforts are boosted by members of the HMS *Cavalier* Association who visit the destroyer for at least one working weekend a year. It is a mutually beneficial arrangement whereby they enjoy the chance to go down memory lane with their old shipmates while contributing to *Cavalier's* long-term preservation.

Left: The aerial for the medium frequency direction-finder mounted on the starboard side of the deck house amidships.

THE AMIDSHIPS IS DOMINATED BY THE ELEGANT raked funnel and large deck house which are flanked either side by the ship's boats. The deck house's features include workshops, stores, air intakes for the two boiler rooms and the point of access to the machinery spaces down below. The large open space immediately aft of the deck house was occupied by a quadruple set of torpedo tubes until the 1964–66 refit in Gibraltar.

Bottom left: The number on each side of *Cavalier's* funnel changed whenever she was reassigned to another flotilla or squadron. She concluded her time in commission as a member of the 4th Escort Squadron. Thus, in keeping with the Historic Dockyard's policy of presenting *Cavalier* in her final guise, she carries a large metal '4' on both sides of her funnel

Below: As part of the funnel's restoration it was capped with metal plating to prevent rain water running down into the ship. Previously, a canvas cover had been fitted over the top and as it deteriorated it developed a number of leaks, so triggering further corrosion within the ship.

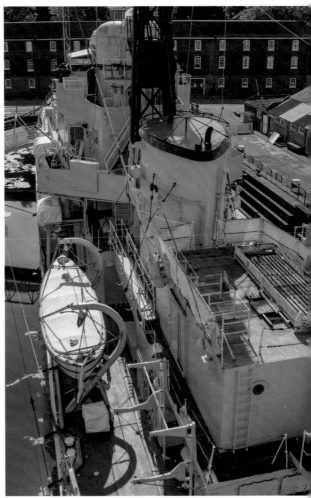

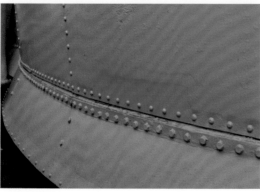

Above, left and right: Detail views of *Cavalier's* funnel, of riveted construction and supported each side by a forestay and backstay.

Above right: The final set of quadruple torpedo tubes was mounted on this deck amidships until it was removed during the refit of 1964–66 to help offset the weight incurred by fitting the Seacat missile system. The general purpose davit on the port side is the last visible reminder of the tubes, originally used both to load the tubes and for the recovery of practice torpedoes. In rough weather this deck would frequently be awash, forcing the ship's company to use the flying catwalk to move between the forward and aft superstructures. At times, even this could be too dangerous to cross, thereby stranding some men aft. In these circumstances, the emergency galleys were used to keep the men sustained until the conditions

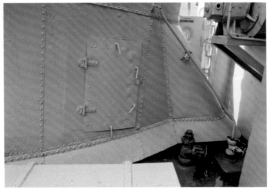

improved. The 25ft motor cutter can be seen on the starboard side, slung in the manually operated davits. Despite the absence of electric winches, launching was relatively easy and involved two to four men using ropes round bollards. In contrast, hauling the ship's boats back on board was a labour-intensive process that absorbed up to 150 men split into two groups co-ordinated by a petty officer. The only woodwork to be found on the weather decks can be seen along the edges of the green-painted steel. Known as the 'spurn-water coaming' it consists of a 1in batten held in place by studs and plugs, and was to prevent stains developing along the side of the hull as a result of rain water or spray running off the weather decks. Instead the water was kept on the deck until it reached a gap in the coaming where it could flow through a rubber chute clear of the ship's side.

THE SHIP'S BOATS

THERE IS AN OLD SAYING IN THE NAVY THAT A ship is known by her boats. Therefore, their crews had to remember that their actions always reflected favourably or badly on the ship as a whole. *Cavalier*'s core complement of a standard Admiralty 27ft whaler and a 25ft motor cutter was supplemented by a supporting cast of smaller boats, including sailing dinghies, which changed during her time in commission. The two principal sea boats were slung on quadrantal davits ready for lowering at short notice.

Right and below: This 27ft GRP whaler is similar to the one that would have been carried by *Cavalier* and was acquired by the Historic Dockyard in 2008. The original was a wooden, clinker-built version capable of being sailed, rowed or used under power that led to it being known as the 'three in one'. Whenever *Cavalier* acted as the plane guard for an aircraft carrier, the whaler would be fully manned and turned out ready to be lowered to assist a ditched aircraft in the event of an accident.

Bottom: The whaler's stern-hung rudder.

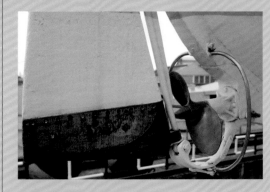

Top: This wooden motor cutter was embarked in *Cavalier* during her time in commission. It could carry up to twenty-six men and reach a top speed of 7 knots. The 25ft clinker-built boat has two cabins and became the principal ferry for the ship's company whenever the destroyer was secured to a buoy or at anchor. Her restoration was completed in 2007 with the bulk being carried out by long-standing volunteers Michael (Mick) Keir BEM and Peter MacDonald, who both died two years later having started the whaler's restoration.

Above: Each boat carried the ship's badge on the bow for easy identification when coming alongside another warship.

Right: The motor cutter's stern-hung rudder.

Above: A raised fo'c'sle, just forward of the amidships section, was incorporated within the design of all the destroyers built for the Royal Navy from 1903, up to and including the *Daring* class of the early 1950s.

Above right: A replica of the ship's bell was presented to the Historic Dockyard in September 2005 by Mark Caroe, who was responsible for the engraving and wax-filling of the its inscription in his own workshop. The bell can be seen amidships in the same spot where the original hung during *Cavalier*'s time in commission. In addition to recording the destroyer's name and year of inaugural commissioning, the original bell would have had the names of all the children who were born to serving members of the ship's company and baptised using the upturned ship's bell as a font engraved along the inner surface of the sound ring. The decorative bell rope was made by a former chief boatswain's mate of the Type 23 frigate HMS *Kent*.

Right & bottom right: The small compartment on the port side of the amidships deckhouse that was used as the diver's store.

Below: The majority of the information plates along the edge of the weather decks were stolen before *Cavalier* arrived in Chatham and have been painstakingly recreated by some of the volunteers.

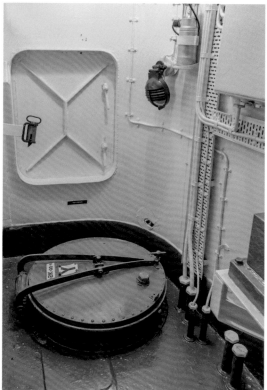

Above & right: This small workshop is located on 2 deck within the deck house amidships. The watertight manhole hatches (right) provide direct access to the machinery spaces.

Below: Three photographs of the battery charging room, situated within the starboard side of the amidships deckhouse, it was used for the maintenance and charging of the batteries for the emergency lanterns that were scattered at strategic locations around the ship. Several batteries could be charged at the same time by placing them in racks above the workbench.

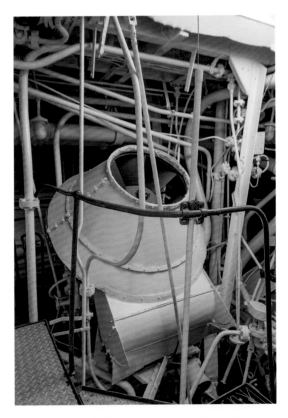

THE HISTORIC DOCKYARD HAS YET TO RESOLVE
the challenge of how to open the machinery spaces to
the public without making significant alterations to
their appearance. These compartments consist of two
boiler rooms, an engine room and the gear room.

Left: The forced draught fan would have been connected to
an air-intake trunk that ran up to the large grills in the side of
the amidships deckhouse and supplied the powerful draught
of air required to burn the fuel in the high powered boilers.

Below left: Pressure gauges.

Bottom left: The left-hand telegraph controls the number of
burners in use while the right-hand one is the engine
telegraph.

Below: In contrast to the other machinery spaces, A boiler
room is bathed in natural light via the grills in the side of the
amidships deckhouse.

Opposite top: The Admiralty type three-drum water tube
boiler in 'A' boiler room. It usually took about four hours to
raise enough steam to get underway. Each boiler essentially
consists of two equal-sized water drums that are connected by
rows of steel tubes, known as generator tubes, to a larger
steam drum above them to form an inverted V shape above
the furnace which is lined with fire bricks. Eight oil fuel
burners are fitted to the front of the boiler and supplied the
Furnace Fuel Oil (FFO) under pressure to the furnace where it
was burnt. As the FFO burned, the combustion gases passed
upwards and boiled the water circulating in the generator
tubes to create super-heated steam at a pressure of 300lb per
square inch. This collected in the upper steam drum and was
piped through to the turbines in the engine room which drove
the propeller shafts via the reduction gearing in the gear room.

Opposite below: One of the two water-level gauge glass
mountings that were mounted either side of the steam drum
to monitor its water level.

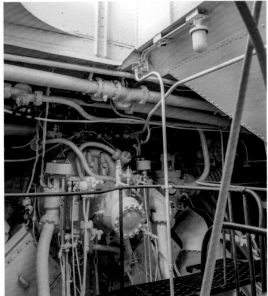

Opposite far right: The engine control position and main throttles in the engine room.

Middle left: The bank of pressure gauges for the steam turbines in the engine room.

Left: One of the manhole hatches that leads down to the machinery spaces.

Right: Each of these wheels opened and closed the valves that controlled the flow of super-heated steam to the engines.

Below: The gear room contains the reduction gearing fitted between the engines and the propeller shafts to manage the transition from the very high rotational speed of the turbines to the comparatively sedate pace of the propellers.

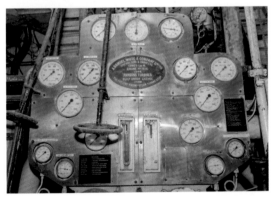

Below: In time, the volunteers will tackle the refurbishment of these telegraphs in the engine room.

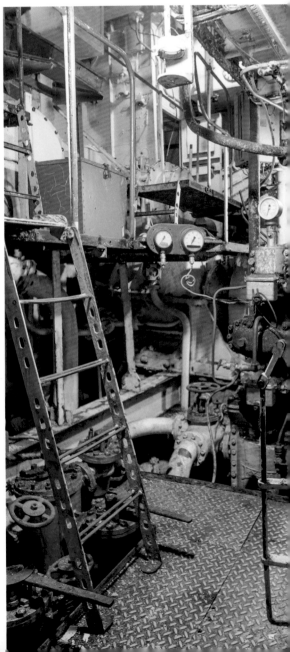

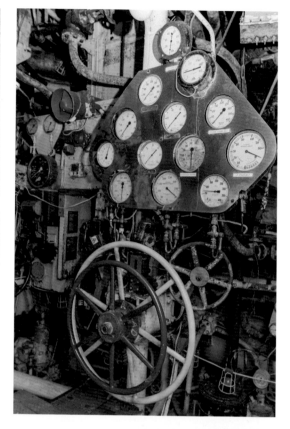

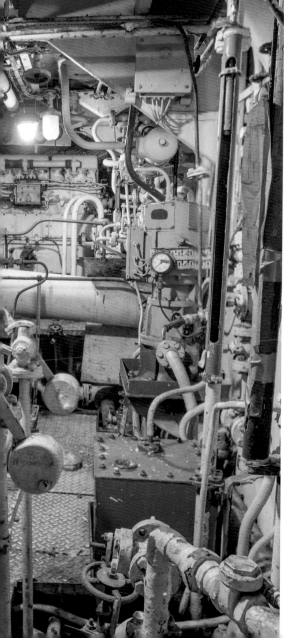

AFT SUPER-STRUCTURE

Alterations to the composition of *Cavalier*'s main armament triggered significant changes to the aft superstructure during the refits of 1955–57 and 1964–66.

THE FIRST SET OF CHANGES TO THE AFT SUPER-
structure were implemented during *Cavalier's* 1955–57 modernisation following the removal of X mounting and the aft set of quadruple torpedo tubes. The aft superstructure was extended forward and topped with a twin 40mm Bofors Mk V mounting and a Simple Tachometric Director Mk 2 on a new raised deckhouse, while the space formally occupied by X mounting was taken up by a pair of triple barrelled Squid ahead-throwing anti-submarine mortars. Further changes occurred during the 1964–66 refit when the twin 40mm Bofors was replaced by the GWS 20 Seacat missile system. This resulted in the addition of a raised deckhouse at the forward end of the aft superstructure to accommodate the magazine for the missiles. To compensate for the additional weight of the new structure, the remaining set of quadruple torpedo tubes were removed.

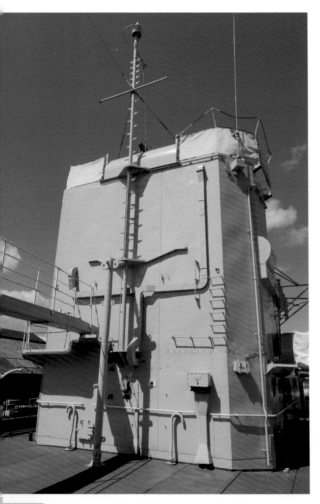

Above: An overall view of the aft superstructure with the dominant raised deckhouse in the foreground.

Left: The upward extension of the aft superstructure's forward end created a rather stark-looking tower. The clear deck, where the last remaining set of torpedo tubes had been mounted, exaggerated the height of this new structure which gave a slightly unbalanced look to the ship's revised profile.

Right: A watertight ready-use shell locker situated on the port side near Y mounting.

Far right: Volunteers work their way round *Cavalier's* brightwork, including this scuttle, on a regular basis to ensure she looks shipshape.

Above: The installation of the Squid anti-submarine system included the addition of a raised deckhouse to accommodate the Squid handling room in which the projectiles were stored. The 390lb bomb-shaped projectiles sank at a rate of 43ft 6in per second and were effective to a depth of 900ft.

Left: looking forward along the starboard side weather deck towards the motor cutter.

Below: In the event of the compass platform being knocked out of action, *Cavalier* would have been commanded from this emergency conning position situated immediately ahead of the Squid anti-submarine system.

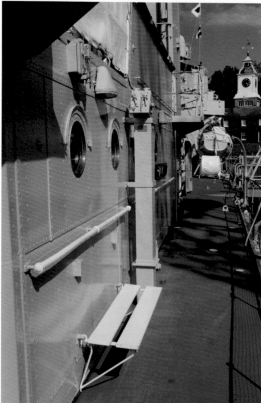

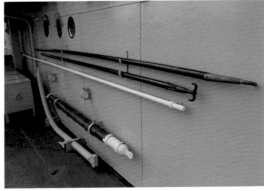

Above: A weatherproof speaker, set of switches and the top of a section of trunking for the ventilation system mounted on the starboard side of the aft superstructure.

Above: Three boat hooks and a wooden boom mounted on the port side of the aft superstructure. The boat hooks were stowed in this exposed position because they could be reached very quickly whenever they were required.

Below: One of the deck lights on the starboard side of the aft superstructure mounted above a telephone handset that provided a direct link, via the intercom, to the compass platform when required.

Below: Looking aft along the weather deck beside the starboard side of the aft superstructure.

Above: Originally, five members of the CA class were due to be fitted with the Seacat Guided Weapons System Mk20 (GWS20). Of these, *Cavalier* and *Caprice* were the only two ships to actually receive the system while the aft superstructures of *Cavendish*, *Carysfort*, and *Cambrian* were modified to take the system. The development of the shipborne surface-to-air Seacat missile system began in the 1950s as a replacement for the 40mm Bofors which had been used by the Royal Navy since 1942. The Seacat GWS20 consisted of a separate four-round launcher and visual director. Capable of engaging targets between 1,500 and 5,000 yards, a rocket booster propelled the Seacat to a speed of Mach 0.6. On conclusion of the boost phase, during which the missile could not be controlled, it would glide for approximately 3,000 yards before rapidly losing speed and falling into the sea.

Right: The Seacat's visual director was manned by two operators and is mounted above the magazine for the missiles. The aimer used a powerful pair of sighting binoculars to track the missile's progress towards its target while making any required adjusts to its course with a thumb joystick control. These movements were converted into command signals and transmitted to the missile via the launcher.

Left: The aerial situated between the four missiles transmitted the signals from the aimer to the missile.

Above: The Seacat magazine, located within the raised deckhouse at the forward end of the aft superstructure, contained a total of eighteen Seacat missiles, consisting of ten operational ones, four used for practice and another four for drill.

Left: Dummy Seacat missiles were usually placed within the launcher to enhance the ship's appearance whenever *Cavalier* entered or sailed from a port.

THE Mk6 SQUID

THE TRIPLE-BARRELLED ANTI-SUBMARINE mortar system was brought into service at the height of the Battle of the Atlantic in May 1943. The ahead-throwing system represented a significant step change in comparison to the depth charges previously used by *Cavalier*, because sonar contact could be maintained while launching an attack. Squid was fitted to destroyers, frigates and corvettes in either a single or double configuration. The removal of *Cavalier*'s X 4.5in mounting enabled two sets of mortars to be installed during the 1955–57 modernisation. Squid was used in conjunction with *Cavalier*'s Type 147 and 164 sonar which provided the target's predicted depth, bearing and range. The three 12in mortar barrels were angled differently to scatter the projectiles so that they formed a triangular pattern approximately 275 yards ahead of the ship. When all six barrels were fired together, the projectiles formed two separate triangles 60ft apart in depth which caused a lethal pressure wave to crush the target's hull.

Above: Each Squid had its own set of rails on which a trolley moved the projectiles for loading. The curved layout of the rails beside the pair of Squids can be clearly seen.

Opposite near right: One of the bomb-shaped projectiles sitting on the trolley that was used to move the Squid's projectiles from the Squid handling room to be loaded in the appropriate tube. When loading the mortar tubes, they would be turned to the horizontal position. On reaching the appropriate tube, the top of the trolley would be rotated so that the projectile could simply be pushed back into the tube.

Right: This large wheel was used to turn the three barrels to the horizontal position prior to the loading of the projectiles.

Top and above: The port side Squid. *Cavalier*'s official badge is mounted on the upper and lower stainless steel covers of the mortar tubes. However, the middle cover bears the ship's unofficial badge

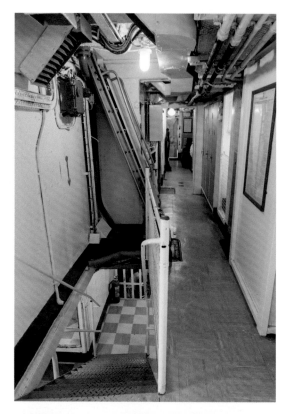

Left: Looking aft, down the main passageway, on 2 deck. The galvanised staircase leading down to 3 deck was fitted after *Cavalier* became a museum ship.

Below & bottom: *Cavalier*'s compact medical facilities were contained within a single compartment and included two pivoting cots. The restoration of *Cavalier*'s sick bay received a boost in 2005 when Commodore Reed OBE RN presented a collection of medical equipment to the ship on behalf of the Institute of Naval Medicine. The compartment's restoration was also assisted by members of the Royal Navy Medical Branch Ratings & Sick Berth Staff Association.

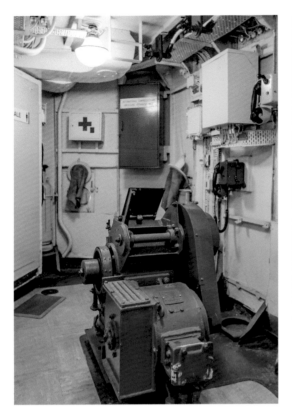

Above: This ammunition hoist brought up the 4.5in cartridges from the magazine for the use of Y mounting.

Below: Instruction plate fitted on the ammunition hoist.

Above: The placing of a foot on the red pedal operated the hoist. At the end of the lifting cycle from the magazine, the 4.5in shell or cartridge would end up on a metal plate from where it was then passed through one of the ammunition hand outs in the aft bulkheads to the waiting gun crew.

OPERATORS INSTRUCTIONS

① HOISTING BY POWER—
RETAINING PAWL AT TOP OF HOIST IN HOISTING POSITION.
SCREW DOWN RAMP AT BOTTOM OF HOIST BY MEAN OF HAND WHEEL.

② HOISTING BY HAND—
REMOVE EYE BOLTS ON MAIN DRIVING PLATE ATTACH HANDLE & SECURE BY SAME EYE BOLTS - TIGHTEN WITH TOMMY BAR

③ EMBARKING—
FIT HANDLE AS FOR HOISTING BY HAND.
STOW RETAINING PAWL AT TOP OF HOIST.
RELEASE LOADING RAMP AT BOTTOM OF HOIST BY HAND WHEEL

④ MAINTENANCE—
BEFORE WORKING ON HOIST LOCK PEDAL
SWITCH BY MEANS OF PIN ON PEDAL SHAFT.

Above: Looking down the flash-tight chain hoist that brought the 4.5in shells and cartridges up from the magazine.

Right & opposite: The opening of the aft compartments in October 2009 provided disabled access to the ship for the first time and enabled the Historic Dockyard to launch 'Crash Out On *Cavalier*'. This educational initiative enables groups of up to thirty youngsters and six adults to spend a night in one of *Cavalier*'s restored messdecks. The package includes an exclusive tour of the ship along with an evening programme of naval activities led by a member of the museum's staff. Since its launch, the Historic Dockyard has managed to secure bookings each year for the majority of weekends from the end of March to the end of October.

Below: This magazine supplied the 38½lb brass cartridge cases for Y mounting. They were stored in these rows of open-ended metal tubes. A metal retaining clip ensured that each cartridge remained in its tube until it was required. When the time came, each cartridge would be moved by hand from its metal tube and loaded into the flash-tight chain hoist which brought it up to 2 deck where it would be passed through one of the flash-tight ammunition hand-outs in the aft superstructure by Y mounting to a waiting member of the gun crew to be loaded at the appropriate moment. *Cavalier* typically carried the following quantities of ammunition for her trio of 4.5in guns: 400 semi armour-piercing (SAP) shells, 600 high effect (HE) shells, 100 star shells, 120 practice shells and 1,000 cartridges. When the Admiralty adopted 4.5in guns it anticipated that they would be the largest calibre to use fixed rounds of ammunition. However, early experience in the cruisers HMS *Scylla* and *Charybdis* proved that the combined weight of 85lb for the shell and cartridge was too much for the gun crews to handle without difficulty, especially in rough weather. Knowing that the smaller size of a destroyer would increase the scale of the challenge faced by gun crews in hostile conditions, the Admiralty decided to initiate the development of 'separate loading' 4.5in ammunition for use on the destroyers armed with this calibre of gun, including *Cavalier*.

Top left: This bathroom is now used by members of the youth groups that sleep overnight in *Cavalier*.

Middle left: This messdeck is now used as the dining hall for the youth groups that spend the night in *Cavalier*.

Lower left: The restoration of the aft messdecks included the installation of a lift to provide disabled access to this part of the ship. This plan initially raised eyebrows among old salts, yet the discreet position of the lift away from the main messdecks has had no real impact on this part of the ship. In addition to allowing disabled youngsters to spend time in the ship, it has enabled some frail veterans to see more of the ship than would have otherwise been possible. The lift can be seen on the left, while the cabin which has been adapted for disabled people can be seen directly ahead.

Right: The tiller flat is reached via this manhole hatch on the quarterdeck immediately aft of Y mounting.

Bottom left: *Cavalier*'s two propellers have a diameter of 10ft 6in and turned at over 300 revolutions per minute as she reached 31 knots. They were both removed when she became a museum ship. For many years this propeller was displayed amidships under the flying catwalk. The other one is preserved on a plinth in Cowes, Isle of Wight, as a lasting tribute to the men and women of Samuel J White who built her.

Below: This compartment provides access to one of the plummer blocks fitted to the starboard side propeller shaft. These blocks support the weight of the shaft to prevent it sagging. These compartments are checked regularly by the volunteers to ensure *Cavalier* is not taking on any water.

Above right & centre: The steering position within the wheelhouse on 01 deck operated transmitter rams which relayed the wheel's movements by pumping hydraulic fluid to and from the telemotor receivers in the tiller flat. These signals were in turn transmitted via mechanical links and levers to the hydraulic rams which worked directly on to the rudder crosshead. The telemotor system proved to be more reliable in action compared to electrical systems. The buckling of bulkheads, decks or flooding usually resulted in the failure of the electrical system owing to broken wires, whereas the telemotor system pipes tended to stretch and bend rather than break.

Below right: The gaps between the empty storage racks, next to the steering gear, provide a good view of the hull's structural components including the frames, stringers, bracket plates and deck beams.

Below: This hatch, within the forward bulkhead of the tiller flat, provided access to the spirit room which, as the name suggests, is where the rum was stored.

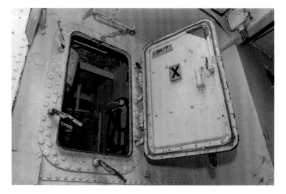

Above and below: The 4.5in Y mounting.

Below right: Once the 4.5in shells and cartridges had been brought up from the magazine, they were manhandled from the ammunition hoist and passed through one of the flash-tight ammunition hand outs in the aft superstructure immediately ahead of Y mounting. A member of the gun crew would take hold of the shell or cartridge as it was passed through the port and stand in line ready for his item to be loaded.

Bottom right: The watertight hatch on the left-hand side of the image provides direct access to the tiller flat.